Published simultaneously by Teachers College Press, 1234 Amsterdam Avenue, New York, NY 10027 and the National Art Education Association, 1916 Association Drive, Reston, VA 20191

Copyright © 2009 by Teachers College, Columbia University

Library of Congress Cataloging-in-Publication Data

Mulcahey, Christine.
   The story in the picture : inquiry and artmaking with young children / Christine Mulcahey ; foreword by Maxine Greene.
      p.   cm. — (Early childhood education series)
   Includes bibliographical references and index.
   ISBN 978-0-8077-5007-0 (pbk : alk. paper) — ISBN 978-0-8077-5008-7 (cloth : alk. paper)
   1. Art—Study and teaching (Early childhood)   2. Inquiry-based learning.   I. Title.

   LB1139.5.A78M85 2009
   371.5'044—dc22

                                                                2009019589

ISBN: 978-0-8077-5007-0 (paper)
ISBN: 978-0-8077-5008-7 (cloth)

Printed on acid-free paper
Manufactured in the United States of America

16   15   14   13   12   11   10   09   8   7   6   5   4   3   2   1

EARLY CHILDHOOD EDUCATION SERIES
Leslie R. Williams, Editor

The Story in the Picture

INQUIRY AND ARTMAKING WITH YOUNG CHILDREN

Christine Mulcahey

Foreword by **Maxine Greene**

TEACHERS
COLLEGE
PRESS

Teachers College, Columbia University
New York and London

National Art Education
Association

Contents

Foreword

READING THIS BOOK is like moving through a looking glass into an unfamiliar art gallery. The walls are hung with the works of recognized, largely modern works of art, interspersed with works by young children between 3 and 5 years old. The atmosphere is neither hushed nor solemn, as it often is in galleries. The wary responses ("beautiful"; "practically like Dali"; "like our house at the beach") so commonly heard have given way to childish voices caught up in conversations with what they see. They might, as the author points out, be finding stories in the paintings. They might be noticing colors, diverse shapes—an elephant, a cradle, a building crane. A child may become a docent, pointing out—in a child's picture or in a Warhol—details of form and color, resemblances, connections.

Dr. Mulcahey is eloquent about the significance of integrating experience with the arts with the experiences of learning, of noticing, of creating. She is clear about the repressive effect of recipes, of copying. She stresses the need for a variety of materials. She offers helpful advice to parents uncertain how to react, how to talk about the artworks children bring home. The book includes a rich assortment of children's drawings and paintings. Christine Mulcahey's watchwords are freedom, creativity, and imagination. She enriches our conceptions of pre-kindergarten curriculum. One can almost feel perspectives opening on her side of the lookingglass as children's voices break through the hush, and we come in touch with the unexpected.

—Maxine Greene

Acknowledgments

ANY PROJECT such as this has several background players participating to make it a successful endeavor. The children I teach, who are referenced in the following pages, are the primary participants, without whom the book would not have been written. Their enthusiasm, their curiosity, and their willingness to experiment, explore, and take risks provided the impetus for sharing their learning with others. Parents and guardians readily gave permission to use their children's photos, conversations, and artworks, and I thank them for their supportive comments.

Thanks to the staff of Teachers College Press, particularly Marie Ellen Larcada, for guiding me through the multiple stages of authorship with patience and direction and for believing in the importance of art for young children.

Copyright representatives for the artists' works pictured in the book were more than helpful with granting permissions and documentations. Many thanks to Alexandra Batsford for permission to use the work of Chuck Close; Cristin O'Keefe Aptowicz from Artists Rights Society (ARS) for permission to use the work of Jean Arp, Jean Dallaire, Paul Delvaux, Henri Matisse, and Rene Magritte; Julie Green from the David Hockney Studio; and Jane Whannel for permission to use Mary Cassatt's work from the Burrell Collection at the Glasgow Museums.

Additionally, I thank my colleagues who teach young children for their infectious wonder and interest in how children think and create, as well as the administration at Rhode Island College for granting me a semester's leave to research and write. I also thank the International Association of Laboratory and University Affiliated Schools for funding to support copyright permissions and the purchase of reproductions.

Of course, there are those players who don't know they are players, who were, and continue to be, helpful in personal ways. I am grateful to Rich for his very special care and encouragement, and to my mom, Helen, for her ongoing support and for her propensity to ask lots of questions, be a good listener, and inspire her children to do the same.

Introduction

"THAT ONE IS SCARY." "It's an octopus!" "It's a big hand." "It's sliding down the mountain!" These were some of the comments the 3- and 4-year-old children shouted out as I showed them the reproduction of one of Jean Arp's abstract paintings. They were clearly transfixed by the colors and shapes, and they had plenty to say about it. I listened carefully as they continued their discussion about what these colors and shapes reminded them of.

I thought of the day, years ago, when I was assigned to teach art to these children as part of my teaching duties at the laboratory school of Rhode Island College, where I am an art specialist and full-time professor. I was concerned at first. Although I had worked with students from kindergarten through college age, I had never worked with 3- and 4-year-olds in schools. How could I keep their attention? What were they capable of doing? I wondered about ways I could help the children learn the same aesthetic and artistic values that I taught to the rest of the children, but yet provide it on a developmentally appropriate level.

I needn't have been concerned. These young children were clearly capable of more than I had previously thought. Their enthusiasm, their observations, and their keen sense of interpretation were, and are still, amazing. My time with them is now the most enjoyable part of the school day. They love looking at artworks, they love talking about them, and they learn from each other at the same time that I learn from them. They have changed my perspective on teaching young children.

This book is about providing early childhood teachers, preservice teachers, parents, and caregivers the skills, and the freedom, to design rich and open-ended art experiences for young children. It focuses on looking at the work of a variety of artists and ways to use these artworks as taking-off points for conversations and creativity with a range of materials. While I present examples of activities I have done with children, these activities set the groundwork for others that you, as teachers, will gain confidence designing on your own, as it fits in with your curriculum.

When children look at works of art, whether it be adult art or child art, they tell stories, share experiences, imagine, and explore. Conversations and subsequent art-making activities become a social activity, as the children interact and learn from each other. It's not necessary that we, as adults, understand a painting or a sculpture that we might share with children; we can learn along with them. I often show reproductions that I know nothing about, and I am surprised by the children's different perspectives on what the artist might be trying to do. The children's responses guide me in determining a "rich" art activity to follow.

Although the field of art education recognizes the value in engaging children with works of art and the social dimensions of artmaking, the field of early childhood education is not as strong a proponent (Kindler, 1996). This book is a way to help bridge that gap.

Learning through and with art treats the visual arts not as a separate discipline, but one that can fit in with an already established early childhood curriculum, or which can be extended for use in the home environment. The lesson ideas are easy to implement, practical, and teacher-friendly. Although the book is a cohesive whole, chapters can also be read and utilized in isolation.

Research in the book is based on personal research and documentation, as well as on research and standards put forth by the National Art Education Association (NAEA) and the National Association for the Education of Young Children (NAEYC). Although both of these organizations support a rich and varied art education for young children, the NAEA specifically mentions viewing and learning from adult artworks, while the NAEYC does not. One of the nine core values and beliefs of the Early Childhood Art Educators (ECAE) Issues Group of the NAEA purports that early childhood art programs should be comprehensive in scope, including opportunities to respond to art through conversation, storytelling, play, dramatics, movement, music, and artmaking.

ORGANIZATION OF THE BOOK

I initially lay the groundwork for working with artists and artworks, and the benefits for young children in doing so. I also discuss why open-ended activities for children result in learning and decision making, referring back to the NAEYC standards and the NAEA standards.

I suggest lesson ideas according to the concepts that may either already exist in the early childhood curriculum or be related to art in general. Every lesson idea has latitude to change into something else based on the interests of the children.

Chapter 1 provides the rationale for using artworks in the early childhood curriculum. I discuss the importance of art history and aesthetics, and how exposure to artworks created by adults and others is educational for young children because it allows children to construct their own meanings, teaches diversity, fosters thinking skills, and encourages storytelling through the sharing of personal experiences.

One of the important components to creating artwork is making sure that the activity allows the child to "think like an artist." Too often, art activities are designed in such a way that all children have to do is to follow directions. I discuss in depth what thinking like an artist means, and I also clarify terminology used in working with artists and artworks (e.g., *realistic, abstract, nonobjective*).

Chapter 2 stresses the idea of open-ended art experiences for young children. Drawing on actual experiences, I discuss the limitations of using traced imagery and precut or predrawn shapes in teaching, not just in art but in other areas of the curriculum as well. I also discuss what a "rich" art activity is and how to make sure that the art you do with your children is "rich."

Chapter 3 opens the discussion of how to use exemplary artworks with young children. I focus on how to talk with children about adult-made artworks as well as about their own artworks. I cover remarks and responses that adults typically make to children, and how to better respond to a child artist. I show actual artworks and discuss sample questions and answers.

My college students indicate that this is one of the most helpful topics of my college teaching. They learn to provide meaningful responses to children when they show their caregivers their artwork, instead of "Oh, that's beautiful!" I discuss responses that help children learn more about the visual arts, albeit in a developmental manner.

Chapter 4 presents actual lessons I have taught and conversations that have occurred between children and me. I focus on the art concepts of line, shape, and color, since they are basic building blocks. I recommend reproductions to use, and I include many photographs of children working.

In Chapter 5 I present lessons I have used to complement and support activities in the preschool curriculum, such as friends and families, letters and numbers, and the manufactured and natural worlds.

I believe looking at different kinds of art will help children be more open-minded and accepting of diversity as they mature. You will learn along with your children, and perhaps become amazed by the children's interesting and perceptive discussions. This approach is not difficult and can be adapted for any teaching situation. So, enjoy this journey, learn along with your children, and explore!

CHAPTER ONE

Why Teach Through Art?

WITH SO MUCH emphasis today on the quality of education, many teachers might determine that including more art-related activities in their curriculum is too time-consuming and unnecessary. And that is understandable, given today's educational climate with its emphasis on accountability and testing. Many teachers of young children use art in their curriculum as a change of pace, as a break from the "important" things. Art is fun, creative, relaxing, imaginative, and helps develop certain skills. What many people, teachers and parents alike, don't know is that using art in the curriculum can go way beyond traditional art teaching, and can provide so much more for children.

In the early childhood classroom, emphasis is often placed on art production, or on "making things." Little time is spent looking at art and learning through art. However, my years of teaching as well as recent research show that children are not naive viewers of art. They are keen observers and are eager to talk about art.

Much has been written about how the arts can contribute to children's lives (for excellent examples, see Davis, 2005; Egan, 1999; Eisner, 1994, 2002). I do not wish to reiterate these beliefs here, but to add to them. By teaching through art, I mean to use recognized adult-created artworks as a learning prompt with children. The actual creating part is an accompaniment to the initial prompt and supports it. Both are important. Using works of art with young children also satisfies the fourth standard in the National Visual Arts Standards: Understanding the visual arts in relation to history and cultures.

LEARNING THROUGH AND WITH ART

As young children look at exemplary artworks, they naturally discuss them. They construct their own knowledge by telling stories of what might be happening in the artworks. They may also share personal experiences of ideas or events in their lives that they are reminded of by viewing various artworks. By doing this, the children learn from each other, they learn about themselves, they learn from their teachers, and their teachers learn from them. Learning through art becomes a social activity, not an isolated, individual activity, such as solitary painting at an easel might be.

Children's social interactions profoundly influence their cognitive development. As most educators know, learning and developing do not occur in isolation. They are dependent on social interaction, and social learning actually leads to cognitive development (Vygotsky, 1978). In school and other early childhood settings, children talk to each other all the time, they share experiences and stories, and they closely observe and learn from each other.

In addition to allowing for more social interactions, talking about art strengthens vocabulary skills and contributes to visual literacy. Thompson (1990) reviews the literature supporting the proposition that language is an essential component of early artistic development, and suggests that appropriate forms of dialogue may provide a foundation for understanding and facilitating early artistic activity development, crucial to the nature and nurture of visual expression.

Research in developmental psychology suggests that young children are more capable of art appreciation than we allow them to be (Gardner, 1990). If engaged in a meaningful conversation about artwork, young children display a surprising amount of sensitivity. They notice different styles and can understand how an artist might think.

While many people think that creating art is a solitary activity, in fact artists have been learning from each other for centuries. Artists constantly view each other's work, converse about artworks, look at exemplary artwork of the past and present, and learn from all of them. The informal gatherings of eighteenth- and nineteenth-century French salons are perfect examples. Artists would gather regularly, discussing ideas and their artwork. In many cultures artists create together, from the quilts of Gee's Bend in rural Alabama, where quilt-making skills and aesthetics have been passed down for six generations, to the Adinkra cloth designs of Ghana. I believe children should be learning that same way. As Vygotsky (1978) points out, children readily learn from their more capable peers, and talking about art is no exception.

INTRODUCING WORKS OF ART TO YOUNG CHILDREN

Teaching young children ways to look at art, talk about it, and appreciate it is not the intimidating task it might originally appear to be. Young children are eager to engage in conversations about artworks, whether it's about their own art or someone else's. Using reproductions of artworks in your curriculum is surprisingly easy and provides a broad range of benefits for children in addition to the benefits that creating art provides. Introducing artworks to young children:

- Allows children to construct their own knowledge
- Teaches appreciation of diversity
- Fosters imaginative and critical thinking skills
- Encourages storytelling
- Allows children to share personal experiences

Constructing Knowledge

As children view works of art, they will naturally interpret what they see based on their personal experiences and their previous exposure to artworks. It is important to accept their interpretations even if it is not what the artist intended (Hohmann & Weikart, 1995). This helps children feel safe and allows them to take more risks in sharing their observations and opinions. If a group of children view an abstract painting, and one sees a dragon, and another sees a bird (Figure 1.1), it's important to listen to them rather than correct them. They have good reasons for their beliefs, which make perfect sense to them.

Figure 1.1. *"This* is a bird!" this 4-year-old says emphatically.

Original Herbalist's Staff in High Museum of Art, Atlanta. All photos by the author.

Children's initial responses to viewing artworks are primary. This allows children to construct their own meanings about what they see, a developmentally appropriate approach (Durant, 1996; Savva, 2003). When children construct their own knowledge they become active participants in the learning process, rather than passive ones. Constructivism is basically a theory about how people learn. It says that people construct their own understanding and knowledge of the world through experiencing things and reflecting on those experiences. When we encounter something new, we have to reconcile it with our previous ideas and experiences; we become active creators of our own knowledge.

By engaging in an exploration of looking at and creating art (Figure 1.2), children and teachers alike explore their own way of learning and viewing the world. Exploring the arts departs from an assembly-line approach to learning and resists efforts to get away from the holistic nature of things (Moore, 1995). Children who react to challenges when presented with new information by asking why and by exploring many possible answers learn far more than those who simply accept facts, figures, and other teacher-directed activities.

When I show children various works of art, I may show one, two, or three reproductions. The children immediately start to talk about the works. My first question is usually "What do you see?" Naturally, there are different responses, depending on what is meaningful for a specific child. We

Figure 1.2. Preschoolers eagerly discuss a Chuck Close self-portrait.

Chuck Close, *Self-Portrait* copyright Chuck Close, Courtesy the artist.

listen to all responses and talk about why we think the picture is about a particular topic. The children engage in conversation, which coincides with Vygotsky's (1978) theory that learning is a socially mediated activity: The children are learning from each other.

When I showed a group of preschoolers Paul Delvaux's *Trains du Soir* (see Chapter 5), the children had several different perspectives. For one child, the little girl in the lower right corner of the painting had significance, for another it was the nighttime, and for another it was traveling on the train. The children read their own experiences into the work, so each perspective was valid. By putting their thoughts and ideas into a discussion of Delvaux's painting, the children will more easily remember the work at a later date. This agrees with Bruner's (1962) theory that children will more readily remember experiences if they organize their thoughts and ideas in terms of their own interests and cognitive structures.

Donaldson (1978) also believes that learning begins with a person's "human sense," which is that understanding of the world we have constructed through our experience. In order for children to learn, they must be able to relate what they are to learn to their understanding of the world. If what is presented to them is distant or irrelevant to their human sense, it will simply be minimally available. Thus the social, emotional, and cognitive experiences a child brings to the classroom are considered part of the learning process (Simpson, 1996).

While the children discuss the artworks, I usually do not interrupt. I do ask questions, which are designed to tell me more about what the child is thinking or what makes the child respond in a certain way. I sometimes add factual information when it does not interrupt the free flow of ideas and when it can contribute to a greater understanding of the artist, the work of art, or another child's perspective (Burnham, 1994). The factual information is usually in the form of a story or it is a quick statement or question. For example, I might mention that Kandinsky liked music and wanted his artwork to look like music sounded, or that Picasso was sad and so used "sad" colors. But the primary emphasis is on the children's construction of knowledge.

Appreciating Diversity

From looking at and learning about the visual arts, children learn a respect for diversity as they look at how different artists use the same theme but create different artworks. Looking at artwork from a variety of perspectives can help children become open-minded and accepting of diverse ways of thinking (Greene, 1995). Everyone has a different way of perceiving the world; by looking at the work of different artists, children and adults can see that there are multiple perspectives and that difference is good and exciting. I believe that being knowledgeable in the visual arts helps both children and adults be more open-minded and accepting of differences in many areas. If children are exposed to artworks at an early age, they will be more accepting of diversity in later years. In fact, in my teaching, I find that the children are more open-minded than some teachers and parents because they have been exposed to such diverse artworks early in their education.

In one conversation with third graders, the children and I were looking at a self-portrait of Frida Kahlo. Some students giggled at her "unibrow" and her "moustache." One student defended the painting by saying that she thought it was beautiful, and that if they lived in that culture, they would think it was beautiful too. The other children accepted this explanation and later were more respectful of this difference in cultural beliefs. By talking about their values and beliefs, children can communicate the similarities among us as well as the differences.

As educators and parents, we need to provide "increasing numbers of opportunities for tapping into long unheard frequencies, for opening new perspectives on a world increasingly shared" (Greene, 2001, p. 189). In our global economy we need to understand that there are many ways of doing things and many ways of seeing the world. Children are often better at this than adults. Looking at art from different cultures can help us see these different perspectives.

One of the powerful aspects of the visual arts is its ability to give us a view of people from the inside out, rather than from the outside in, illuminating the world of human feelings, perceptions, and values (Johnson, 2002). Literature does this as well, but visual images are immediate and taken in more quickly, particularly by young children who do not yet know how to read. Suzanne Langer (1942) describes this as discursive vs. nondiscursive. In a discursive form, as in literature, meaning is made from a sequential sequence of words (discourse). The complexity of the discourse is limited by what the mind must retain from the beginning to the end. In a nondiscursive form, or the visual, meaning is taken in simultaneously. There is no sequential order of viewing. It is immediate. Learning through art is learning a different source of knowledge, one that is becoming more and more prevalent in our society with the use of video and digital imagery, touch screens, and other forms of visual stimuli. When we view a work of art, or a computer screen, or advertisements, we take in the visual aspects of the image all at once, a difficult task indeed. When we listen to a story or read a book or article, we take in a word, a phrase, a sentence, and eventually the entire text, and need to remember the sequential ideas. Both of these "readings" are important to learn and master.

Fostering Imaginative and Critical Thinking Skills

Even at a young age, students should be learning how to use their imaginative and critical thinking skills, skills that will help them as they face life's most complex tasks (Eisner, 1985). Learning through art, where there is no one correct answer to a problem, provides opportunities for learning these skills, as well as for learning different perspectives, alternatives, and multiple solutions to problems, or the kind of learning that Maxine Greene (1995) suggests should be the goal of education itself.

Imagination is a cognitive capacity that is often ignored in education, and yet it is fundamental to learning (Greene, 2001). Many of us may think that imagination is just dreaming up fantasies or false hopes. But with imagination come wonder, inventions, and discoveries, not just in art, but also in life. Dewey (1934/1980) spoke of imagination as the capacity to look at things as if they could be otherwise. Imagination opens new worlds, discloses new vistas, and makes life enjoyable.

When children look at artworks, they might imagine what is happening in the picture, or what happened before or after. They can put themselves in the picture and discuss how they would feel or what they might do. Describing what they see in an artwork, beginning to interpret images, and discussing why an artist would paint in a certain manner is a start to using critical thinking skills.

Kieran Egan (1999), a noted educator and writer on children's thinking and learning, believes that the development of the imagination is crucial and that education should strive to engage children imaginatively. In fact, a child is much more imaginative than an adult. As an example, Egan gives a box to an adult and to a child and asks them to think of different uses for it. Typically, an adult will give up "after a few minutes with six uses, [but] the child is into the 50th and just warming up" (p. 87). However, as children get older, imagination and play take a back seat in education, and, unfortunately, education turns to more "serious" things.

Part of developing the imagination is using metaphor. Whereas logical tasks are often difficult for young children, they will show remarkable ease and flexibility in dealing with the complex logic of metaphor (Egan, 2001). This is important because it "seems tied to the active, generative, imaginative core of human intellectual life. There is in metaphor a logic that eludes our analytic grasp" (p. 16). In fact, research shows that our ability to recognize and generate appropriate metaphors reaches its peak by age 5, and then declines (Gardner & Winner, 1979; Winner, 1988). When the children I teach viewed Jean Arp's *Configuration*, they quickly came up with several metaphors of what the yellow shape was. College students, on the other hand, often had few metaphoric descriptions.

Humor also plays a part in talking about art. Viewing humorous art lets children know that not all art is serious. And, of course, it isn't. It is important to foster a sense of humor in young children (Figure 1.3). Egan (1999) believes that stimulating and developing a sense of humor are ways of helping provide a foundation in logic and philosophy, where skills in arguing, thinking, and analyzing are basic. When I joke with the young children I teach, which I do often, they are quick to interpret the humor. They respond with jokes of their own and call me "silly." But they easily distinguish the difference between what is serious and what is not.

Encouraging Storytelling

Stories engage children powerfully, particularly stories that are related to fantasy. Looking at artworks helps children learn how to tell stories as they relate their own experiences to what they are seeing. Storytelling encourages active participation, higher level thinking, creative thought, and expression of emotions (Wellhousen, 1993). It also helps to enhance linguistic fluency and build self-esteem (Peck, 1989).

When children view artworks, they are quick to tell a story. The story could relate to a real event in their lives or an imaginary one. One child may begin the story and finish it, or another child may pick up a thread and continue it.

Figure 1.3. Aimee displays her sense of humor as she feels and shapes pieces of clay.

Egan (2001) believes that the story was perhaps the most important of all social inventions, because it provided the bond for people to form more complex societies. When people did not have a written language, oral stories were the only way to pass down the history and traditions of the culture. Even today storytelling has the potential to elicit emotional responses. And emotional responses are essential to learning (Caine & Caine, 1994; Egan, 1999; Sylwester, 1994). How much easier is it to remember events associated with emotions? Grandchildren sit at their grandparents' feet listening to stories about the "olden" days. We easily remember a lost love, a happy childhood memory, a sad movie. These stories and events, which are connected to emotional responses, are more easily stored in memory and thus more easily retrieved.

Allowing Children to Share Personal Experiences

Goodman (1978) proposes the view that humans construct their own worlds and no one world is more privileged over another. By sharing their worlds with each other, children learn about their peers, they learn about artists and artworks, they learn about possibilities and events. And teachers learn as well. Children are eager to participate in discussions that revolve around their own experiences (Thompson & Bales, 1991). They easily introduce members of their families, past and future events, and values that they and their families hold.

Children are far more sophisticated than we often acknowledge. Duncum (2002) maintains that much of education fails to recognize the realities of children's lives and the emotional sensitivity they possess. By sharing personal experiences, children demonstrate their ability to look into others' lives as well as their own, and to respect the right of others to also share their experiences. Using artworks as an impetus to sharing personal experiences also coincides with Freire's (1970) belief that education is not neutral—that we bring our backgrounds, values, and beliefs to the classroom and share them in the act of communication. Discovering what children know and what they believe profoundly influences what they learn (Siegler, 1991).

UNDERSTANDING AESTHETICS

Aesthetics is a vague area that we don't think about often. Maxine Greene, Emerita Professor of Philosophy and Education at Columbia University, is a luminary in the field of aesthetic education. She shares her vision of the power of the arts in education to transform student indifference into a state of "wide-awakeness" (Greene, 1995).

Young children already have that "wide-awakeness" that Greene talks about, but it needs to be fostered by aesthetic inquiry to continue throughout life. Aesthetics stresses the perception and appreciation of qualities, rather than the study of science and facts. In a broader sense, *aesthetics* means perceiving or feeling something through our senses of touch, taste, smell, sight, or hearing.

The Aesthetic Experience

When we perceive or feel something through our senses we have an aesthetic experience. An aesthetic experience invites imagination and can be one of the best kinds of learning that schools can offer (Greene, 1995). Having an aesthetic experience is the result of being deeply affected by sensory perception, which in the long run increases our cognitive abilities. In understanding aesthetics, we are engaging with the external experiences in the world and the wonder of life. This sensitivity does not come naturally. By learning to attend to the variations of art and life, we may find a deeper presence within ourselves and within our world. As a result of this awakening of our imaginations, passions, and curiosity, we gain understanding (Greene, 2001).

Although the proper content of school curricula should be located in the world in which children live, this is not often the case (Eisner, 1994; Goodman, Smith, Meredith, & Goodman, 1987; Greeno, 1989). Outside of school, children use other senses to explore. Splashing in a puddle and gleefully watching the droplets of water, or looking at the colors produced by drops of oil in the puddle are aesthetic experiences children engage in naturally. In schools, however, teachers unknowingly limit the possibilities for perceiving by allowing only two sense organs to be used; the eyes and ears are overworked in schools as the other senses are neglected (Goodman et al., 1987).

Aesthetics in Art Education

When children talk about art, they are beginning a journey into aesthetics. In art education *aesthetics* is defined as understanding the nature of art through a variety of concepts (Lankford, 1992). These concepts address all aspects of art: responding to art, working with process and product, questioning what art is, discussing why artists create, reflecting about art, looking at the beauty in art, and others. It is an ongoing discussion and there are no definitive answers. Aesthetic inquiry allows children and adults to explore the meanings of these concepts and how they relate to the larger world.

Aesthetics, like all philosophical inquiry, is based on wonder. Philosophers wonder about things most people take for granted. Young children do the same until their sense of wonder is deadened by socialization, education, or some combination of the two. They reach a plateau in their sense of wonder and their willingness to express wonder—often around the fifth or sixth grade—when they also reach a plateau in drawing development. Perhaps, if we focus early on allowing wonder and fostering the desire to explore situations that may have no definitive solutions, children would not reach these plateaus. Young children joyfully engage in meaningful discussions of complex problems and situations.

When children discuss works of art, aesthetics easily enters into the conversation. I ask the children questions dealing with why they think the artist created a work or what they think the work means, as they fit in with the conversation. We explore the aesthetic qualities of lines, shapes, and colors. In one lesson the children and I explored qualities of line. We used strips of yarn, clay, wire, and natural materials such as straw, iris leaves, and grasses. They looked at and described them, felt them, folded and cut them into pieces, and some children made them dance in the air. They followed the movement with their eyes and delighted in the paths that they made. They laughed joyfully. In one class a 4-year-old non–English speaking boy held a piece of fuzzy yarn in the air and danced it around (Figure 1.4). It stood upright, floated downward, and spun around in circles. Its flow and movement through space seem to mesmerize him. His actions

Figure 1.4. A non–English speaking child "dances" a piece of fluffy yarn.

were that of a graceful ballet dancer, and I wondered if he had taken dance lessons. All of these are examples of children responding aesthetically.

Children's aesthetic potential is inherent and natural, but it must be cultivated through adequate social and verbal interactions (Lim, 2004). Aesthetic development is seen as a social and cultural process rather than a fully natural or biological maturation (Vygotsky, 1978), and so needs appropriate language to support children's emerging artistic intelligence.

When children and I discuss works of art, we respectfully listen to each other's opinion. We do not attempt to come to a consensus about what a work of art says or means. Coming to a consensus does little to encourage reflective thinking or dialogue, which is exactly what we want to promote in young children. By listening to their peers, children can build up a collection of ideas that will enable them to more clearly see and eventually appreciate a variety of perspectives.

Is aesthetic inquiry important? I believe it is. It allows children to focus on ideas and issues that go beyond art, the classroom, and the school. It involves looking at a variety of meanings and trying to bring them to a coherent whole. It also promotes equity in that it gives equal emphasis to each child's thinking based on the reference point and experiences of the child.

Unfortunately, learning in aesthetics is not measurable, and parents and colleagues are not aware of its existence unless a specific notice goes out to inform them. It is up to us, as teachers, to educate parents and our colleagues as well.

THINKING LIKE AN ARTIST

In any art activity we do with children, it is important to ensure that the children are asked to think like an artist. In Figure 1.5 I summarize four aspects of "thinking like an artist."

Artists often look at things more closely than most people do. They tend to notice things that others might miss, often with the eyes of a child. For example, while driving or walking, they may notice the stretch of telephone wires against the sky as the wires converge and then separate. Or they may see the nuances of color in objects or reflections. They are curious about many things, much like young children are curious.

Artists also tend to look at things in different ways, often without using labels. Labels categorize objects and people and often get in the way of really "seeing." When artists sit down to draw or paint a scene or person or still life, they look at the objects as shapes and lines, not as trees or noses or chairs. They notice how the shapes and lines are related to each other;

Figure 1.5. Thinking like an artist.

What does it mean to think like an artist?	*Why should we think like an artist?*	*How do we think like an artist?*
We look at things more closely than most people do.	We find beauty and complexity in everyday things and situations.	We look, think, feel, smell, touch, and enjoy the world.
We look at things in different ways.	We learn that everyone sees the world differently.	We explore how different artists and cultures create art.
We take risks and keep an open mind.	We gain confidence that anything is possible; we learn about ourselves and others.	We experiment and try new ideas and materials.
We dream and imagine.	We strengthen our imaginative and critical thinking skills.	We tell stories, and think about what could be, rather than what is.

they look at spaces between shapes; they look at shadows and how the shadows relate to the object; they see light and note its source. Artists also are aware of the many different styles and genres of art, understanding how different cultures use art for different purposes.

Artists often take risks with their work since more will be gained by taking a risk than not. We expose ourselves to risk any time we begin a work of art. Children do the same. Will it turn out the way they want it to? Will they be able to control the paint? What if they don't like it? Most young children don't worry too much about these concerns, but some will. Older children will often be more concerned. As teachers, we need to reassure the child that risk is a good thing and that mistakes are learning experiences. It's OK to change your mind and change the plan. Taking risks may be frustrating, but much more will be learned—about yourself, about the medium, about your ideas, about many things.

Keeping an open mind and not judging prematurely is an important skill in thinking like an artist. As a work of art begins, the final outcome may be planned, but there is always the potential that something could happen along the way to change it. Many changes may occur during the process. Yes, most artists have a plan and do innumerable sketches, but there is always the unexpected drip of paint or brushstroke or chisel movement that can alter the plan. Young children are often nonjudgmental about their own artwork. They gladly switch courses without judging their motives or their progress. Four-year-old Stephie said she was going to draw a hippo and began drawing, only to change it into something else as she progressed. Carl sculpted a charming dog, and then smashed it and created something else. Older children are not as flexible. They often worry about what the final product will look like and become discouraged if it does not.

Along with taking risks, artists are constantly asking "what if." What if I use a different color, what if I use this oil pastel with paint, what if I drip the paint on rather than brush it on? They are constantly thinking about new ways to see and new ways to use materials. They imagine, they dream, just as young children do. If all children do is follow directions, they are doing none of these things.

CONCLUSION

In my teaching I have found that children love looking at and discussing works of art, and sharing their stories with each other. When appropriate, I supply pieces of information about the artist or about what the artist was trying to achieve in the artwork. However, my goal is more about showing children the variety that exists in the art world and allowing them to talk, rather than supplying them with knowledge. The research of Douglas, Schwartz, and Taylor (1981) suggests that children's interest in making art is increased if adults encourage them to talk about art and artists—who artists are and how they make things. Children then understand more how artists think and how they create work from a variety of perspectives.

Although art-making activities are common in most early childhood programs, talking about adult artwork is not. And linking conversations about artists to children's art-making experiences is rare indeed (Epstein & Trimis, 2002; Savva, 2003). Children benefit, teachers benefit, and learning is enriched.

Art Activities for Young Children

"So, WHAT KINDS of art activities do you have planned for the children this week, Kathy?" I asked a colleague and friend as she set up her classroom on Monday morning. "Well, I thought I would just let the children paint whatever they want at the easel, and then I have a snowman project for them to complete," she replied. She showed me her easel area where there was a selection of paints and a stack of paper. Then she showed me her snowman area where she had assembled cut-up pieces of foam and pipe cleaners so the children could assemble snowmen since it was a cold and snowy day.

We chatted briefly, and I went back to my classroom to prepare for the day. I thought about Kathy's planned activities. I was a little confused. She was providing two completely different activities for her preschoolers: One was free and open, and the other was scripted. How unfortunate for her children whose early exposure to art would be limited by these types of experiences.

This dilemma is common in schools and preschool settings. With so much emphasis on avoiding patterns and predetermined outcomes for children, teachers are confused about what kinds of experiences to provide. On the one hand, they think that allowing children to paint or draw freely is an answer to this dilemma; on the other hand, they still provide controlled activities for their children because it's what they know. They assume that a teacher-controlled activity would be a good balance with the free painting activity. While these approaches do provide a balance, they are at opposite ends of a continuum: One is too open and one is too closed.

ACTIVITIES THAT ARE TOO OPEN-ENDED

A free painting activity provides little structure: Children are free to do what they want and when they want. Is this bad for children?

While this is not a "bad" activity, it can be greatly improved upon. Children do need time to focus on expressing their own feelings and ideas.

Some children, however, when presented with a blank piece of paper need a theme or idea to get them started. Blank paper is sometimes intimidating to a young child. Many older children will often say, "I don't know what to do," when presented with a blank sheet of paper.

Free painting at an easel is also a solitary activity. While children need free time by themselves, they also need time to share and learn from their peers and teachers. Learning through art can be a social activity. It can be a time for telling stories and for rich conversation as described in the previous chapter. It is the perfect time for discussions about artwork, which allow for social and cultural factors and which recognize the significance of scaffolding and teaching, proposed by Vygotsky (1978) 30 years ago.

ACTIVITIES THAT ARE TOO CLOSED

Although much has been written about avoiding patterns and predetermined outcomes for children, some early childhood teachers still lapse into providing controlled activities for them. They make patterns for children to trace or color or paint; they provide step-by-step directions for creating a product; or they give all the children the same materials and they all create the same thing at the same time. These are all recipe-oriented activities. Why are some teachers still doing this? I believe there are several reasons: Teachers can control the activity and the outcome; teachers often feel inadequate regarding art knowledge; teachers do not know how to respond to the creative process; teachers feel that being creative is a talent you either have or do not have.

Teacher Control

A recipe is comfortable for teachers because they know exactly what to expect: They know what the product will look like; materials can be organized ahead of time; materials remain neat and tidy; and cleanup is quickly and easily done. It is unfortunate for the child, however, because without any input from the child the activity is not self-expressive or creative. In fact, it's not art at all!

As educators help children become independent learners, we want our children to be able to think for themselves, to be able to make decisions, and to act on those decisions. But by providing a step-by-step art activity, we are not allowing young children to make decisions nor are we teaching them to become independent. A creative art opportunity allows children to begin choosing and seeking knowledge on their own, giving them more and more confidence in their own abilities. Art, where there is no one correct answer to a problem, provides opportunities for learning these skills, as well as for learning different perspectives, alternatives, and multiple solutions to problems, or the kind of learning that Maxine Greene (1995) suggests should be the goal of education itself.

Little Art Background

Many people feel inadequate regarding their art knowledge. Most of us do not have a strong background in the visual arts. Because most teachers of young children have little background in art, they often fall back on their previous art experiences in elementary school. Many of those activities were craft oriented, pattern determined, and teacher controlled. As Elliot Eisner (1988) asserted 20 years ago, teachers do what they know how to do. If teachers' early art education was limited to coloring ditto sheets or creating teacher-prepared craft projects, then this practice will continue until teachers are convinced that better alternatives are available and they are more enriching than what they have already experienced.

Art discoveries are central to the education of young children, but teacher preparation in this area is minimal. Approximately 75% of colleges and universities require only one course in the visual arts for preservice teachers, and others require none (Jeffers, 1993). In some colleges students often take one course that covers music, art, and drama, hardly enough to make a beginning teacher feel confident.

Response to the Creative Process

Teachers, caregivers, and parents often do not know what to say to children who show them their paintings, drawings, or sculptures. But conversations with children about their art-making endeavors can be a rich, description-laden opportunity. Talking to children about their artwork sends subtle messages about the value that is placed on art. And again, because beginning teachers do not have much of an art background, they don't know what to say, so they often resort to comments like "I love it!" or "That's just beautiful!" There are many more educational ways to talk to children about their artwork, which I discuss in detail in Chapter 4.

Talent in Art

Are people born being creative or artistic, or is it something you can learn? In the courses I teach at the college level, most students initially say you can't learn it. However, when I take them through many different draw-ing exercises and introduce them to artistic thinking, by the end of the semester they are thinking differently.

Research shows that being able to draw is a teachable, learnable skill (Edwards, 1999). Yes, it takes time, and, yes, you need the desire to want to learn. In many classrooms, I hear teachers say to me as well as to their students, "Can you draw this for me? I can't draw at all!" This sends a subtle message to children—there are those who can and those who can't. It may very well be the case that you, the teacher, never learned how to draw or how to see things artistically. But, with time and effort, it is possible. Why not say to children, "Well, Damien, you can learn how to draw and think like an artist. I wish I had done that when I was your age." This lets chil-dren know that it is possible. If teachers believe that drawing or creativity is an unreachable talent, their children will believe that also. The hidden curriculum is a powerful influence.

THE IMPACT OF COLORING BOOKS
ON CHILDREN'S DEVELOPMENT

In a college class I teach, I talk about using coloring books with young chil-dren. "Oh, I just loved coloring books!" several of my students exclaim. When I ask them why, they tell me that it is relaxing, it's repetitive and soothing—and you don't have to think. Yet they can't possibly imagine why it would be detrimental for children!

Simply put, coloring books are adult-generated images designed to occupy children's time. Teachers sometimes use these methods so they can accomplish work of their own while the children color. Although coloring in books *can* be relaxing because children are not required to think to com-plete the work, do we want children *not* to think in school? Activities such as these often make children dependent at a time when children should be learning independence. Children can become so accustomed to seeing adult-generated images that when asked to create drawings of their own, they become frustrated because their work resembles that of a child—as it should—rather than that of an adult. When children become frustrated, they lose interest in drawing and the creative process.

Some teachers rely on predrawn images, which they ask the child to either add to or complete by coloring them in. One teacher I know requires an extensive book report from his fourth graders, and then provides a pic-ture for the children to color in for the cover. How much better it would be if the children chose part of the story to illustrate themselves.

In another situation, a preschool teacher takes her class on a field trip to an apple orchard. In the classroom afterward she cuts out big apple shapes for the children to paint with red paint. What is the child learning by doing this activity? It's not really necessary to cut specific shapes for children to paint. Allow the children to have some choice as to paper and paint. And, after all, not all apples are red!

THE IMPACT OF TRACING

- A third-grade teacher teaches ancient Greece in her curriculum. The children research Greek culture and art. She passes out maps for the children to trace.
- A kindergarten teacher has plastic stencils of letters, numbers, animals, and other cute figures. At free-choice time, the children eagerly trace them and color them in.
- A fourth-grade teacher supplies cutouts of the parts of a skeleton for his children to trace and cut out. Then they follow his directions to put them together with cotter pins so that the joints move. He hangs them all around the room—every one of them is the same.

The above scenarios might appear to be a small thing to the classroom teacher, but when combined with many other similar experiences, they send a subtle but powerful message to children: Children are unable to draw and so need adult-created images to trace or copy.

Tracing serves little purpose. Like coloring books, it makes children dependent on adult-drawn images, when children should be learning independence. When something is traced it results in a false sense of pride; it is really no accomplishment for the child. Some teachers will say that it helps fine motor control, but a stencil actually serves as a guide for a pen or pencil and children use fewer small muscles than they would if they drew or scribbled on their own. Also like coloring books, tracing can result in children becoming frustrated when asked to draw on their own.

Tracing maps does not teach much about a country. Children will not remember the contour or shape of a country by tracing a cutout of it. They will remember it more if they look at a picture in a book and try to draw it on their own. That way, they will be making comparisons, looking at proportions, and utilizing more of the right side of the brain. In other words, they will be thinking! Children learning about the bones in the body will remember more if they actually look at a model of a skeleton and draw from observation. Even young children can learn to draw from observation. Of course the result won't be perfect, but more about the object will be learned and remembered, which is the goal in the first place.

Jan, a good friend and colleague of mine, approached me one day to discuss what she was doing in her third-grade classroom. The children were reading *Stellaluna* (Cannon, 1993), and she thought she would have the children make bats. She mentioned giving them a pattern to trace. Of course, I was shocked when I heard her say "pattern." "No, no, no!" I countered, "You can't possibly let them trace a pattern!" "But I don't really have a lot of time to do much else," Jan replied. I calmly suggested she have the children study bat anatomy and then allow them to make their own bats using a variety of materials. Reluctantly Jan agreed.

A few weeks later Jan came into my classroom, and said, "Chris, you have to come in and see the bats. They are adorable! The children have been working on them a little bit every day." She was so excited because the children had been so inventive with their creations. She told me that the children had researched bats and learned about their habits and diet, the benefits of having bats, and stories from bat lore. They used lots of materials to create their original bats. The children loved creating them and each one was different from the next. She hung them all around the room, and she and the children discussed how wonderful they were. Taking this different approach changed the focus for Jan and her children. What the children learned from this activity was now more important than what the children did. Not only did they learn about bats, they also learned how to make choices regarding materials, techniques, and ideas.

This seems like a small concern, but children need to know that adults, both teachers and parents alike, trust that they will succeed without giving them crutches that will eventually affect their artistic confidence and their willingness to try new things.

"RICH" ART ACTIVITIES FOR CHILDREN

I like to think that art activities should be chosen with the same rationale that child development specialists use to recommend and select toys for children: They recommend choosing toys that are open-ended and provide a variety of options for play, such as blocks and Legos (Bredekamp & Copple, 1997). If there is only one way to play with a toy, it is limiting to the child's imagination, and, in fact, children tire of it quickly. Children may prefer to create something different every day with their toys, and this kind of play is more valuable for development.

We can choose art activities with similar ideas in mind: What can children do with this? How can each child come up with a different solution?

What kinds of choices will the child have? Keep in mind that it is important for a teacher not to provide a finished example of an art activity. This will limit the child's ideas. Also keep in mind that "open-ended" activities does not mean that children should have free rein to do whatever they want. By providing motivation and brainstorming for ideas, teachers can help children find many ways to do things.

After viewing and discussing different artworks with children, I follow with what I call a "rich" art activity. A rich art activity has the following characteristics:

- Asking what the children will learn rather than what the children will do
- Connecting to the larger art world
- Allowing the children to make choices
- Asking the children to think like an artist
- Providing for a variety of outcomes
- Avoiding recipe-oriented activities

Focusing on Learning Rather Than Doing

Typical art activities revolve around what the children will *do*. In rich art activities, however, the focus is on what the children will *learn* and how they will learn it, as it is in math or other academic subjects. When I work with practicum students and student teachers, they are often too concerned with the activity itself, the materials to be used, and the product the children will create. When I ask them what the children will learn, they often cannot come up with an answer. How do you distinguish between the two?

As a simple example, in one kindergarten lesson my student teacher wanted the children to paint pictures of animals since they were learning about different animals in their classroom. I asked why he wanted to do that and what he wanted the children to learn. He thought for a while before he answered, "Well, children really like animals, and I think they will have fun painting." I told him that as a future art teacher, he needed to think about more than just providing a "fun" activity for children. I continued to ask him what would the children *learn*? He had a hard time coming up with an answer. We sat for a while and brainstormed.

He decided that he would initially focus on the artwork of Andy Warhol, particularly his prints of endangered species. While he showed several of Warhol's works, he concentrated on the animal prints, which are colorful renditions of endangered animals all created in vivid, unrealistic colors (e.g., an elephant is pink). He and the children discussed the prints for several minutes, bringing in their own experiences with animals, what animals looked like, what endangered meant, and why Andy Warhol used such bright colors. Then the children each created an animal using a variety of materials (Figure 2.1).

What did the children *learn* from this activity? They learned about a twentieth-century artist, Andy Warhol; they learned about endangered species; they learned about animals from their peers and from their teacher; and they learned about art materials, colors, mixing paint, and making choices. The learning that resulted from this activity was much richer than just "painting animals" would have been, and yet the children still had fun.

In a later sculpture lesson, the children viewed paintings and sculptures of animals from a variety of artists. Franz Marc's *Blue Horses*, Alexander Calder's *Cow*, Jean Dallaire's *Birdy*, and Aboriginal animal prints provided a range of realistic and abstract works from different times and cultures. By looking at several artists this time, the children learned that people have different perspectives and that each perspective is valid. Just as different artists produce different results, so do the children (Plate 1).

Connecting to the Larger Art World

The art lessons described above connect to the larger art world because they introduce exemplary artists. In the Warhol lesson, the discussion focused

Figure 2.1. Devon has used many materials to create this composition. Here is his description of his artwork: "I'm making a snowman, and here's a birdhouse. It has three birds, a seagull, a pigeon, and a bluejay. Here's a pond and a birdbath. A fish just jumped out!"

on why an artist would paint in that style. The children were perceptive about Warhol's choice to paint the animals in unrealistic colors (Figure 2.2). When asked why an artist would want to paint in that manner, there were several responses: "Because he wanted us to really look at his paintings; he wanted to use his imagination; maybe the sun was shining on the animals." Without disclosing a lot of detailed information about the artist, the teacher allowed the children to construct their own knowledge about artists and animals, a more enriching experience for everyone.

Making Choices

The children make several choices in these lessons. They choose their animal, the size and color paper to use, the colors of paint or crayons or markers, and how their animal is portrayed (Figure 2.3; Plate 2). Some children chose to create birds or fish or imaginary creatures. They also decide what else they wish to include in the painting or sculpture. The accreditation criteria of the National Association for the Education of Young Children (National Academy of Early Childhood Programs, 2005) indicate that young children should have opportunities to plan and make choices. Here is an opportunity for us to give them freedom to do so. Children, if allowed, are extremely creative and revel in the opportunity to choose materials.

Figure 2.2. Carl draws a "rainbow dog" with lots of little dogs below it. He eagerly describes his drawing: "The baby dogs are red, and when they grow up they change color, just like some birds do."

Figure 2.3. Sharon's animal painting.

The simplest choices for teachers become major decision-making op-portunities for children. What color paper to choose, what color crayons or paint, what shape and size of paper, which way to hold the paper are all options the child should have. Children may require more time to work if many decisions must be made, but the time is well spent. By choosing, children will select different combinations of materials and slowly learn more about the properties of those materials as well as the effect one ma-terial has on another.

Thinking Like an Artist

The previous chapter discussed in detail what it means to think like an artist. In the Warhol lesson described above the children looked at Warhol's animals and discussed why he might have created his prints. They are learn-ing that artists think differently, and that each artist has a different way of showing his or her thoughts and ideas. At the end of class there was a shar-ing of the children's work, and the children could see how each of them provided a different response.

Allowing for a Variety of Outcomes

Needless to say, all the children's work was different. Some children painted or sculpted several animals, while others created only one. Some children included themselves in the picture. There were different backgrounds, different sizes of paper, and different colors of paint. Each child approached his creation differently; there was no right or wrong way to begin or finish (Figure 2.4).

Avoiding Recipe-Oriented Activities

The Warhol lesson is clearly not recipe oriented. Think about the opening paragraph of this chapter, where Kathy is planning her snowman activity. All the children will need to do is to follow directions, think little, and all results will look the same. There is quite a difference between the two.

CONCLUSION

Providing open-ended experiences based on adult artwork gives children a rich exposure to art and a rich exposure to art experiences. Children are learning and doing at the same time. As children look at examples of works of art that initially inspire them, their visual perception skills are being nurtured. Since the preschool child is at the stage where a language system and vocabulary are developing rapidly, it is the perfect time to introduce simple art terms and beginning art knowledge (Douglas et al., 1981).

Figure 2.4. Bobby decides to paint a dinosaur instead of an animal. He adds to it at a later date by using oil pastels.

Allowing children choices of materials and ideas stimulates the imagination and allows the child to think more inventively. A child's personality and viewpoint are reflected in his artwork, and teachers can show respect for the child by encouraging his own way of working with art materials (Colbert & Taunton, 1990). Looking, discussing, and creating together turns an art activity into a social activity where children can all learn from one another. This approach provides rich conversation, allows for social and cultural factors, and recognizes the significance of scaffolding and teaching, as proposed by Vygotsky (1978).

Talking with Children About Art

THIS CHAPTER OPENS the discussion of how to use exemplary artworks with young children. I focus on three areas: how to talk with children about adult-made artworks, how to talk with children as they are creating artworks, and how to talk with children when they have completed work, in order to provide feedback. I give examples of remarks and responses that adults typically make to children, and tell how to better respond. I show actual artworks and discuss sample questions and answers.

My college students indicate that this is one of the most appreciated topics of my college teaching. Instead of saying, "Oh, that's beautiful!" they learn to provide meaningful responses to children, helping children reflect on their creations and perhaps providing new information for the children. We discuss responses that help children learn more about the visual arts in a developmentally appropriate manner.

No matter how much we know about art, it's still challenging to know what is the best thing to say to children about their artwork. We want them to feel good about their creations, and we want to encourage them to continue making art. But we are also busy teachers and have to attend to many things at the same time. What is the best way to talk to children about their artwork?

Much has been written about responding to works of art (see Barrett, 1997; Hamblen, 1984; Housen, 1983; Parsons, 1987; Schirrmacher, 1986). Many of these approaches are subject based, focusing on understanding what the artist is trying to do. Jessica Davis (1993, 2005), on the other hand, focuses on approaching a work of art from the viewpoint of the learner. She proposes asking open-ended questions designed to elicit insights based on what the learner already knows, which encourages the learner to develop and use his or her knowledge independently (2005, p. 144). Basically Davis's technique allows the viewer, or in this case the young child, to construct his or her own knowledge.

Although Davis discusses her method in relation to working with viewers in an art museum, I feel it can be used in any venue, particularly in schools. The approach I have been using for years is similar to Davis's and is designed specifically for working with young children.

BEGINNING CONVERSATIONS ABOUT ARTWORKS

Almost every lesson I teach begins by viewing reproductions of artworks. I may show one, two, or three reproductions, depending on the content of the lesson and/or activity. I usually begin by asking the children, "What do you see?" This question is open-ended, and all children are able to give some kind of answer. This creates a safe environment for engaging with the artwork, and allows the children to construct their own meanings, as described in Chapter 2.

The answers vary: "I see red." "I see a square." "I see a train." "I see a girl." "I see an octopus." Each child's response depends on the lens through which he or she is looking and the developmental age of the child. For example, if Manuel* has just visited his grandmother, he might see a grandmotherly figure in a picture. If Rachel is afraid of the dark, she might notice that first in a painting. Younger children will notice colors, shapes, lines, or expressions first. Older children may be able to look deeper into the artworks and see other things, such as how the background is related to the foreground, or they may be able to find symbolism in the objects portrayed. Each child should be able to respond at his or her level. This will help children feel secure in sharing their thoughts with the group.

In a painting of a bird by Jean Dallaire, I asked the 3- to 5-year-old children, "What do you see?" The responses varied: "I see lots of blue." "I see a dragon." "It looks like a bird." "I see an airplane." "I see a big triangle and some little triangles." Each time a child responded, he or she pointed to the object in the reproduction (Figure 3.1). The children continued talking about the picture. They came to a conclusion that the painting was a bird. The object of our discussion was not that the children all agree, nor was it necessary for them to agree, but in this case, they appeared to agree. I then asked what the artist did to make it look like a bird. Here is our conversation:

MARC: Well, it has a beak (pointing to the triangular beak shape).
STEPHIE: And it has feathers.
RACHEL: It has feet like a bird.
CARL: And it has wings, but they are circles!

---

*All children's names are pseudonyms.

Figure 3.1. Two 5-year-olds point out shapes and objects
in a Jean Dallaire painting, *Birdy*.

Jean Dallaire, *Birdy* © 2009 Artists Rights Society (ARS), New York / SODRAC, Montreal.

CM: Does it look like a real bird?
STEPHIE: No, it's weird!
MARC: It's a dragon bird.
CM: Why do you think the artist painted it this way?
NATE: I don't know.
SHEILA: Because it's fun!
CARL: Because it's his imagination!
STEPHIE: Maybe he didn't want to paint a real bird.

The children were not perplexed or surprised that the artist created an imaginary bird. What always strikes me about the responses of young children is that they are open-minded about accepting an artist's choice to create things in different ways. They never criticize or disparage an artist's portrayal or an artist's idea. They accept everything.

I told the children that when artists create, they often think up a name or title for their work. I asked them what they thought the artist might have called the strange bird painting. The children eagerly tried several names: The Silly Bird, The Dragon Bird, The Blue Bird. Children love to try and guess names for paintings or sculptures. I then told them the actual title of the work, *Birdy*, but did not give them additional information about the artist or the painting, as I may have with older children. If young children want further information, they will usually ask.

I like to make a connection between a work of art and an artist. Asking the children why they thought the artist painted *Birdy* in that particular way introduces them to several concepts. First, there is an actual person who created the work. Sometimes the children will ask questions about the artist, for example, "Where does the artist live?" or "Is it a man or a woman?" This helps them form a mental picture of a person creating the work, and it helps them make a personal association. If I have a picture of the artist, I will show it to the children. Sometimes I will share interesting facts about the artist or the artist's life. Second, the children learn that the artist had a choice for how he wanted to represent a bird. This lets the children know that when they create a work of art, they have choices as well.

I then showed the children another painting of birds, which was completely different from the Dallaire. The Currier and Ives painting of *The Happy Family* shows a family of pheasants, all happily foraging in the forest. Although Dallaire's painting and the Currier and Ives painting are of birds, the styles are quite different; one is realistic, the other is abstract. The children and I discuss these words and their meanings, and in subsequent lessons, we refer back to them. I like children to know that artists have many ways of depicting the world, because I believe it keeps them open-minded and accepting of different points of view.

In one of my preschool classes a friend and colleague stopped in the classroom while the children and I were discussing the terms *realistic* and *abstract*. As the children and I continued our conversation about various artworks, my friend was amazed that the children could articulate the meanings of the words. She told me later that she didn't learn those terms until she was much older. In fact, when I was 4 years old, I didn't know the meanings of those words either.

By showing children a variety of styles and approaches to creating art (Figure 3.2), it lets them know that difference is natural, and that it's fine that their art looks different from the art of their classmates.

If I am showing two or three different artworks, I might ask the children, "What do you see that is the same in each picture?" Or "What do you see that is different?" Again the answers will vary. Some children might point out that the colors are the same, or others might say that the pictures are all of birds. It's important to give every child an opportunity for voicing an idea, no matter how far-fetched their ideas might seem to us.

With very young children, just looking at works of art and pointing out different kinds of shapes or lines will begin a conversation. When discussing a Matisse collage, one child mentioned that the shapes reminded him of the ocean, another said the shapes reminded her of the summer

Figure 3.2. While I was working with the children, these two boys walked up to this reproduction of a Nigerian sculpture. They had a quiet discussion of whether the bird was a crane or a flamingo.

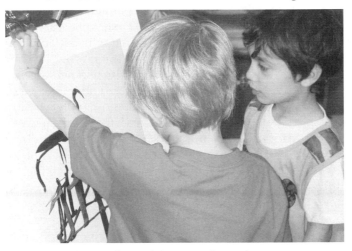

Original Herbalist's Staff in High Museum of Art, Atlanta.

(Figure 3.3). The important idea is that the children are attending to works of art and learning about them and about each other.

CONVERSATIONS WHILE CHILDREN ARE WORKING

Allison, a 4-year-old, had just picked up her paintbrush to create a painting of an apple tree, which her classroom teacher had assigned after a field trip to an apple orchard. She dipped her brush into green paint and spread the luscious color broadly onto her large white paper, clearly intrigued by the remains of thick pigment trailing on the surface. Allison's teacher immediately asked her, "Wouldn't you rather start with brown paint?" Allison looked up at her teacher, hesitated, and then chose the brown paint.

This teacher's remark was based on an assumption the teacher made about the "correct" way to begin a painting. It sent a message to Allison that what she was doing was wrong and that there was a better way. Even though Allison was reveling in the aesthetic experience of the green paint, she then hesitated and began to do what the teacher suggested.

This kind of a response is common from teachers and caregivers. We have expectations based on our prior experiences, and if children don't meet

Figure 3.3. The children find little shapes and big shapes in works
by Matisse and Arp.

Jean Arp, *Composition* © 2009 Artists Rights
Society (ARS), New York / VG Bild-Kunst, Bonn.
Henri Matisse, *Beasts of the Sea* © 2009 Succes-
sion H. Matisse / Artists Rights Society (ARS), New
York.

them, we unknowingly respond with a remark that may discourage a child.
Because the teacher in the above scenario would have painted the brown
trees first, or perhaps because she thought it would be easier, she expected
the child to do the same.

All artists, however, approach their work in different ways. There is
no right or wrong way. One day when I was attending an open studio ses-
sion in which participants could draw or paint from a model, a fellow artist approached me. He told me that he always liked to look at my work at
the beginning and then at the end because my approach was so different
from his and because he could never anticipate its final form. Children are
the same way. We, as adults, need to be open-minded about the different
ways children will begin and finish a work of art, and use words of encouragement rather than falsely correcting them. Just because we might
begin a painting or a drawing in a certain way doesn't mean that a child,
or anyone else for that matter, will use the same procedure.

In Allison's case a different response from her teacher could have made
the child feel good about her choices. There are several responses that
would make Allison feel proud of her work and want to continue paint-

ing. The teacher could have said, "Look at the beautiful green paint!" or "That color makes me think of the apple tree leaves blowing in the wind!" or "I can just smell the trees and the apples!"

The initial response from the teacher may have a tendency to discourage the child from spending more time on her work. After all, why should a child make personal choices if the teacher stands by and corrects her?

CONVERSATIONS TO PROVIDE FEEDBACK

It's the fourth class meeting of my methods and materials for art education class for preservice elementary teachers. We are discussing several children's artworks that I have hanging up on the walls. I point to one and ask my students what they would say to a child who shows them the work and asks if they like it. I tell them to keep in mind three things: They cannot assume what the child has created; they cannot use "I like"; and they cannot use other complimentary words.

My students look at the artwork (Figure 3.4) for about 30 seconds. A few brave ones try some responses. "Wow, you've worked really hard on that!" is one guess. "You must really like the color red," is another suggestion. They continue to look at the drawing. The class grows quieter. They are stumped.

The next question I ask my students is what they think the drawing depicts. There are several responses: a turtle, an apartment building with a lot of windows, a school, a classroom showing desks arranged in rows.

Figure 3.4. Preschooler's "X-ray drawing."

They continue with other responses. I point out the variety of responses—none of them correct—but I still do not tell them what the drawing is about.

The next question I ask them is, "What do you see?" Several of the students begin by saying, "I think I see . . ." but I stop them. I ask again, "No, *what* do you see?" It takes a while, but then the responses come: "I see red." "I see lots of squares." "I see a big rectangle." "I see little circles that are colored in." And the responses continue. I still do not tell them how the child has described the drawing.

This simple exercise reveals how quickly we make assumptions about children's art. The assumptions we make impact our responses.

Making Assumptions

As teachers, parents, or caregivers, we feel a need to know what a child is doing. Because of that we are often quick to make assumptions. It could be natural curiosity or a feeling of wanting to be in control of the situation. But it is not necessary for us to know what a young child is depicting. Their symbol system is different from ours and we may not understand it completely. I have heard stories from college students who were completely turned off by art because of what a former teacher had said to them in response to a work they created. It's not really that difficult to respond appropriately to children's artwork, but it does require practice.

From the new responses my students gave me, I next ask them what they could *now* say to a young child about this particular artwork, keeping in mind the three requirements: They cannot assume what the child has created; they cannot use "I like"; and they cannot use other complimentary words. I also remind them that we are talking about a 4-year-old child.

And so the college students try again. "Wow! That's a lot of squares!" one student responds. Another says, "All your squares are inside a big rectangle." Their responses are getting better, and we continue to push our thinking. I then tell the students that the picture is a truck carrying boxes. The students laugh, and nod their heads, as if it makes perfect sense. And it does! The picture is actually an X-ray drawing that shows a large truck filled with lots of square boxes. The truck is drawn as if you can see through it. This simple exercise demonstrates how quickly we make assumptions about children's art.

I observed a student teacher in a first-grade art class one day. She walked around the room, commenting on the children's work. She looked more closely at one child's drawing and said, "I love your bird in the tree!" The little boy looked up at her with a sad look on his face and said, "That's not a bird. It's a squirrel."

The student clearly made an assumption about what the little boy was drawing, and it affected her comments to him. If the student had stopped, paused, and thought about what she could say, this encounter might not have happened.

Complimenting

I also tell my college students to be careful of too much complimenting of the children's work. It is so easy to say how much we like something because we don't really know what else to say or because we are too busy to really attend to all of the children.

Children often come up and ask me, "Do you like it?" I stop, look, and reply, "Do *you* like it?" They look at their artwork again, and usually answer yes. When children do this, are they really looking for compliments? What is it that they are really asking for? I believe that they are looking for us to *attend* to their work, not necessarily compliment it. And complimenting does not always engage the child in a conversation. It can be a one-word answer.

I find if I comment on something in the drawing or sculpture, the child will most often start telling me about the artwork. In respect to Figure 3.4, for example, if the teacher had said, "I love it!" the child might have just continued working on it without adding comments. Saying, "Wow, look at all those squares!" elicited a description from the child as he described the boxes in the truck. A reflective, stimulating conversation followed. The child was providing more information about his drawing, and he was clearly pleased with it.

I try to tell the children that it's not important if *I* like their work; it's important that *they* like it. Saying something more specific about the work lets the child know that you are really looking at and thinking about it.

WHAT ARE THE BEST RESPONSES?

There is no one right answer for what to say to children when they show you their artwork. But some comments are better than others. The first thing to remember is to make no assumptions. Look at the elements the children have used, such as lines, shapes, colors, and textures. Just saying them out loud is a simple start. Describing the lines or shapes will draw children back into the composition helping them to reflect on what they have created. Some things you might mention are the colors used or the kinds or numbers of lines and shapes you can see. Are the lines straight, curvy, zigzagged, short, or long? Are the shapes large, small, or circular? How did the child use the tool? Was there a lot of pressure or a little? Are there any textures? How would you describe them? Are the brushstrokes long and filled with paint, or short dabs of paint? Use descriptive words to describe what you see in order to give the child more information about what he or she has created and perhaps introduce new vocabulary.

The best kind of comment you can make is one in which the child learns new information in a developmentally appropriate way. For example, children will often mix paint together inadvertently and produce a new color. In one painting, the child had a mixture of colors that, from a distance, looked green. Close up, however, I could see the streaks of blue and yellow. I said, "Wow, from far away, I see green! But when I get closer, I see blue and yellow!" This comment does two things. It lets the child know that when colors are mixed together, they produce a different color. It also lets the child know that looking at work from a distance looks different from looking at it close up. Artists constantly step back from their work to obtain a different perspective.

Another way to judge a good response is to make sure it is geared to only one child. Saying, "You must have worked really hard on that," or "Those colors are beautiful," could be said to any child. It is not specific enough. Your response should show the child that you are only attending to his or her work.

Again, talk about the elements the child has used, how the work makes you feel, or use the artwork as a departure point for an imaginary adventure or story.

CONCLUSION

Most children love to talk about their artwork. There are a few who are somewhat reticent, and they should not be pushed to describe their work. Art does not always need words to accompany it. It can stand alone, and if a child chooses that option, that's fine. Rachel often was reluctant to discuss her drawings, saying, "It's just a plain picture." However, she always took part in other conversations we had and talked with the other children as they were working. Gradually, she began to talk more about her work. Providing appropriate responses helped her to open up to more conversation.

If we compare drawing or painting to writing a story, our response choices become clearer. When a child writes a story, we read it, comment, or ask questions about it; we might ask what will happen next, and so on. We seldom just say, "I like it." We should think of responding similarly to a piece of art.

In the well-known Reggio Emilia schools, children produce artwork of amazing quality. It doesn't just happen, however. Teachers use rich language before and while their children are creating, which stimulates feelings and imagination (Edwards, Gandini, & Forman, 1993). Children are often more imaginative and pictorial than adults, and this rich language feeds their thinking, resulting in a qualitatively diverse array of artworks.

Plate 1. The children were painting pictures of animals. Chaud was not quite ready to paint a realistic portrayal of an animal; he was more interested in the flowing qualities of the paint and the different colors he was using. As he painted, he said, "The animals are hiding!" Not all children are ready to create an image.

Plate 2. Heidi paints a picture of a pink kitty. She doesn't like it and complains that it looks like a pig. I find it charming

Plate 3. Four-year-old Sherri experiments with cutting shapes. Rather than holding up her cutout shape, she holds up the remnant, looking through the negative space.

Plate 4. Lucia creates a jungle scene based on Rousseau's paintings. She uses torn paper, crayon, and oil pastels to finish it.

Plate 5. This young child loved to draw with fine-pointed markers and pencils. He would always find a comfortable position and focus completely on his drawings.

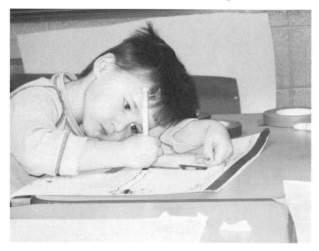

Plate 6. Two preschoolers demonstrate what it looks like to strike a "thinking" pose.

Plate 7. After a discussion of emotions, Rachel draws herself as happy. Her drawing has a carefree, happy look, not just because of the smile on her face.

Plate 8. After a conversation about food, Stephie draws herself about to enjoy a plate of chocolate chip cookies.

Plate 9. Nate first creates a collage of letters and numbers based on the work of Jasper Johns. Then he applies paint on top and uses the end of his paintbrush to etch lines into the colors.

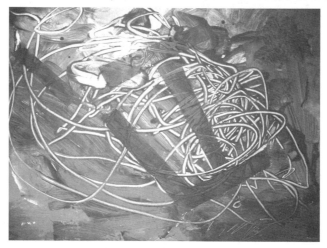

Plate 10. This 4-year-old was fascinated by the blue paint. When she got some of it on her hands, she was intrigued by how it felt and looked. She promptly covered both hands with it, and then began painting on her paper.

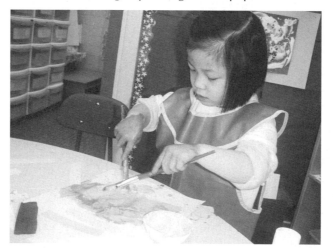

CHAPTER FOUR

Concepts in Art

ALMOST ANY ART reproduction can be used with children. I try to avoid examples of outright violence and explicit nudity. I will, however, show children examples of works of art that depict acts of war, such as Picasso's *Guernica* (an abstract rendition of the Spanish civil war), or other depictions of emotional events or interactions.

Much of what I do fits in naturally with the early childhood curriculum. I will meet with teachers to discuss what is happening in the classroom so I can support it. However, I also include objects of study based on art concepts that I think are important to a child, such as explorations in color, line, and shape and particularly experiences with clay and other forms of sculpture.

Although there are several basic art concepts, I choose to specifically explore line, shape, and color. They are the most developmentally appropriate for young children and the building blocks for subsequent concepts. Young children marvel at the lines, shapes, and colors they naturally explore in their environment, and so a focus on these three elements complements and further enhances their interest in the world around them.

LINES AND SHAPES

I often begin the year by discussing line and shape with the youngest children, ages 3 to 4. Lines are easy to understand and discussions on shapes naturally follow. We explore many different materials, both natural and manmade. We look for lines in our clothing, in the classroom, in leaves, grasses, flowers, shells. Sometimes we make lines in the air with our fingers, or place different pieces of linear materials on top of reproductions to emphasize lines an artist uses (Figure 4.1). We walk and arrange things in lines, zigzag, curvy, or straight. Eventually our lines turn into shapes, by arranging a piece of yarn in a circle or by directing a crayon to draw a free-form shape.

Figure 4.1. Preschoolers fit materials on top of one
of David Hockney's paintings.

Rhode Island Laboratory School class project, October 1, 2006, poster
image is of the David Hockney painting, *Garrowby Hill* 1998, oil on
canvas, 60 × 76", © David Hockney.

Just about any artwork can be used to show children different kinds
of lines. I like to show a variety of artists, so children will become familiar
with different styles, titles, and artists. I also use a mix of realistic, abstract,
and nonobjective works. *Realistic* works of art are depictions of objects as
they appear in everyday life. *Abstract* art depicts realistic objects, but in an
unrealistic way, for example, a cityscape with distorted buildings and
unrealistic colors. A *nonobjective* work of art shows no real objects, but is a
combination of lines, shapes, and colors. For the youngest children, I group
the abstract and nonobjective works together, and call them abstract. With
7-year-old children, I begin to distinguish between abstract and nonobjective. (Nonobjective is also referred to as *nonrepresentational*.)

When we explore lines in an artist's work or in nature, we describe
them by using a variety of adjectives: straight, curvy, zigzag, bumpy, wavy.
The children devise inventive descriptions, and they will often use metaphor to describe a line. Children may describe a line by what it reminds
them of: "That line reminds me of driving on a bumpy road!" or "That line
feels like it's sliding down a hill!" Using metaphor helps develop the imagination, and, as Egan (2001) states (see Chapter 1), children are remarkably
adept at using metaphor to describe feelings or ideas.

Figure 4.2. Katie uses yarn, pipe cleaners, and crayon
to explore lines and shapes.

Any linear material can be introduced, and the children can devise
their own ways of using them (Figure 4.2). Over the years I have used string,
yarn, grasses, leaves, wire, glue, colored masking tape, and crayons. One
day I brought in a variety of leaves to explore. The children waved the
leaves around and made them dance. "They're dancing," I said. "The lines
are dancing!" The children made all the leaves dance in the air as they
smiled delightfully.

As the children danced the leaves around in the air, they could see
how a leaf can change depending on how it is viewed. Sometimes it is wide
and other times it becomes narrow as it is viewed from the side. This is a
sophisticated art concept presented and explored in a simple manner. And
the children were having a wonderful time. One child split his iris leaf into
many pieces, creating several lines. Another decided to color on hers with
an oil crayon. She noticed how more color accumulated near the veins of
the leaf because of its texture. Jeremy took out a stick and drew short and
long lines on his.

Another day we used Model Magic (a soft, white, self-drying clay
made by Crayola) and began sticking various linear materials into it. Anna
pulled off several small pieces of clay and stuck Styrofoam pieces in it (Figure 4.3). She had about seven pieces lined up. She quietly but studiously
worked on her minisculptures.

Devon, on the other hand, made one larger sculpture by sticking linear materials into a base of Model Magic (Figure 4.4). We talked about the

Figure 4.3. Anna carefully pulls apart small bits of clay and pushes pieces of Styrofoam into them to create a series of small sculptures.

"holes" in his piece and about how the sculpture changed when we looked at it from different sides, important attributes of a sculptural form, but presented in a simple manner.

In one of my favorite activities, I brought out several different colors of masking tape for the children to experiment with. First, we discussed lines in different reproductions; then, I talked to them about how some artists use tape instead of paint or crayons to create art. The children were intrigued by pictures I showed them of tape artists at work. They eagerly began cutting and sticking the colorful masking tape on their paper. Some of them enjoyed making a variety of lines, and others created pictures with stories. In Figure 4.5, Carl shows himself and his brother digging for trea-

Figure 4.4. Devon uses all of his clay to build one sculpture.

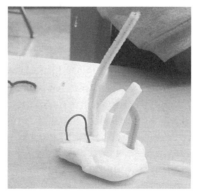

Figure 4.5. Carl uses colored tape to create lines. His lines turn into an imaginative story about digging for treasure.

sure. They have long shovels in their hands, and an X marks the spot for the treasure. He has embellished it with crayon drawings of flowers and clouds. I was impressed with his dexterous use of the tape to depict his treasure hunting.

In another tape drawing, a group of children worked on a mural. They decided what they were going to create, and then they all worked on their small portions, talking excitedly the whole time. Stephie created a gray hippo, her favorite animal. She placed strips of blue sky above the hippo with a yellow sun shining down. Red tape is used for sunscreen on the hippo's body. To the right of the hippo is a rectangular car. Carl says about his car, "It's one of those cars that goes by itself. See? There's no one in it!" Three children worked on the opposite side of the mural, creating a bunny, a princess wearing a crown, and a house.

Using the tape gave the children new ideas about how to create. They plunged right into this novel activity, coming up with new ways to use the medium. They knew if they wanted to create a circle, it would be difficult, and so they came up with another solution. They used other materials as well, such as crayons and markers to add further details to their pictures. There was no right or wrong way to use the tape. The children devised their own problems and came up with their own solutions (Bredekamp & Copple, 1997). They also learned from each other, as they observed and copied ideas from their peers (Vygotsky, 1978).

We, as teachers, need to be risky enough to give children freedom to choose materials and themes. Since children are often more inventive and imaginative than we are (Egan, 2001), they need freedom to be able to choose. Prescribing every activity by teacher standards is detrimental to a child's development into a creative individual. Having a plan is fine, but allowing the plan to change based on the children's interests and needs is more meaningful for the child.

As the children work with lines, the lines naturally evolve into shapes (Figure 4.6). There are many activities in which children can explore shapes, from cutting paper or cloth or natural objects, to drawing shapes, to cutting shapes out of clay, to printing shapes with vegetables, sponges, or cardboard, to finding shapes in nature. There is no right or wrong way. If you are stumped for ideas, ask the children!

Sometimes I show reproductions of paintings with large simple shapes such as Jean Arp's *Configuration* or more complex shapes such as one of Kandinsky's works. The children point to and describe shapes they see and what the shapes remind them of. Again, their stories are quite imaginative. When viewing some of Keith Haring's works, the children laughed hysterically as they made up stories to go with the whimsical pictures. Haring uses lots of bright colors and simple shapes to tell amusing stories. He also punctuates his drawings with lines drawn to show movement or emotion, which the children were quick to understand.

Figure 4.6. Khoury used glue to explore line after a discussion of Jackson Pollock's drip paintings. The white glue dried clear, and then Khoury applied fluorescent pastels over the glue to produce a brilliant, contrasting composition.

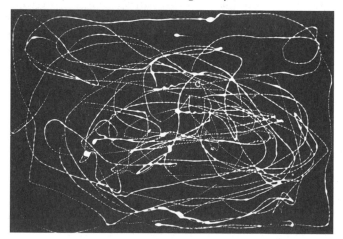

When working with shapes, I like to have many different materials available so the children have choices. Materials that are fun to feel and touch are usually favorites, such as soft fabrics, shiny metallic paper, cellophane, or glittery yarn (Figure 4.7).

As the children work with shapes, we discuss several concepts. We talk about size differences (Figure 4.8), straight and curvy edges, silly shapes, and basic shapes. Sometimes a child will cut a hole out of a shape, and we all take turns looking through it (Plate 3). We count shapes and organize them in different ways (Figure 4.9). These are all basic art concepts and the children are learning them at a young age.

COLOR

Children are fascinated with color. They love looking at colors change as they mix them together. I do very few prescribed activities with color, but instead allow the children to experiment and discover on their own. When children discover how colors change, they are much more interested and will remember more than if a teacher shows or tells them. Experimenting and discovering things on their own are perfect learning opportunities and developmentally appropriate for young children (Bredekamp & Copple, 1997). Too often a teacher will say, "Today we are going to mix colors," and then presents a scripted and controlled activity. I would prefer that

Figure 4.7. Susi explores with lines and shapes in her sculpture. She used different kinds of wire, beads, and yarn on a clay base.

Figure 4.8. Four-year-old Dominic's simple-appearing composition is quite sophisticated. He arranged his shapes according to size and then, with marker, carefully drew a line around them.

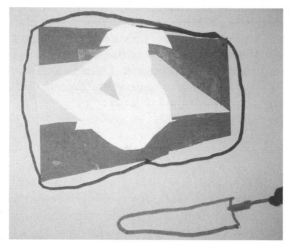

Figure 4.9a. Marc's use of imaginative play is evident in the way his triangle becomes many things, here a moustache.

Figure 4.9b. Marc's triangle becomes a beard.

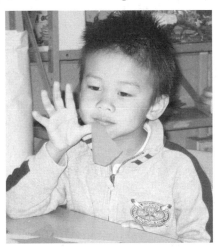

children "accidentally" learn how to mix colors by playing or by doing a painting. This doesn't mean that children should be left on their own to experiment all the time. With guidance and stimulating conversations, their discoveries will become richer.

Almost any colorful reproduction can be used to show the variety of colors in an artist's repertoire. In Kandinsky's works, I might have a child point to all the different reds or blues around the painting. This lets the

Figure 4.9c. Marc's triangle becomes a hat.

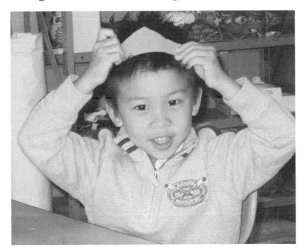

child know that they are spread out all over the painting, not just concentrated in one area, a simple form of balance in a work of art. We also discuss how some reds might be lighter or darker than others. We compare and contrast shapes and colors in a developmentally appropriate way.

Henri Rousseau's paintings are wonderful for looking at different shades and tints of green (Plate 4). Natural objects provide opportunities to explore color up close. Children are fascinated by looking through magnifying glasses at shells, leaves, insects, and other items from nature. We find that white shells are not really white, leaves are not all the same shade of red or green, and apples are not all red.

Children can explore color on different papers, by gluing down shapes and adding color on top of them. They notice how colors change depending on what's next to them and underneath them. By scratching through paint with the end of a paintbrush, different colors are revealed. Any materials can be used, from paint, crayons, and cellophane to oil pastels, markers, and water. Children are inventive enough to choose their own materials and to combine materials as well. I seldom limit the number of materials the children can use. Wonderful results are achieved when crayons, different kinds of paper, markers, and paint are all used together.

One day as I observed a student teacher, I noticed two children fascinated by the changes in their water as they repeatedly dipped their brushes into it (Figure 4.10). Soon all the children were talking about the color of their water. The student teacher said to the children, "Never mind playing with the water; paint on your paper instead." If children are fascinated by

Figure 4.10. Two children delight in the changing colors of their water.

how their water changes, they should be allowed to experiment. Children are sometimes surprised to see that everyone's water ends up the same color at the end of a painting lesson. We discuss why and talk about what colors each of us used. Now they know that when all colors are mixed together, they get a brownish-grayish color!

I often try to sit down with the children to work alongside them. I think it's important for them to see me working as an artist. I can model artistic thinking, and I can exclaim over new discoveries. As I mix colors together, I will exclaim, "Wow! Look at this beautiful color!" They eagerly come over to look and ask how I made it. Rather than telling them, I suggest that they try it themselves. And they do!

THREE-DIMENSIONAL WORK

Children should have ample opportunity to work in three dimensions. They seldom see sculptures unless they have access to a city that has displays of outdoor sculpture, or unless they visit a museum. However, even helping children become aware of architecture can make them see that art is not just painting or drawing or collage. Constantin Brancusi, a well-known sculptor, described architecture as "inhabited sculpture."

I use several different media for sculptures: clay, cardboard boxes, paper, wire, beads, wood, and found objects. Just about anything can be formed into a sculpture.

Clay

Children love clay! They love to feel it, break it apart into little pieces, pound on it, and make things. One of the first things I do with very young children is put out a large block of clay for them to explore. Any air-dry clay is appropriate, as long as it is kept covered with plastic so it does not dry out. At first they are unsure of what to do with it. They look at it and gingerly touch it. Then they become more physical and begin making impressions in it, first with their fingers, then with their fists, gently at first, then more forcefully. Some children break off little pieces, but others like to tackle the entire block.

After a while, I set out a box with lots of objects with which to make impressions, and they eagerly press them into the clay block (Figure 4.11). They take sticks and make holes in the clay, seeing who can make the deepest hole. They stick all sorts of objects in and bang on them in a patterned rhythmic chant, singing and dancing. Then they take all the objects out of the clay, and begin all over again. Katie notices the small impressions, saying in her quiet voice, "Look at the fancy marks."

Figure 4.11. Children love making impressions in a large block of clay.

The children invent wonderful stories about what's hiding in the clay. I facilitate by asking lots of questions. "What do you think is inside the clay?" I ask. They have different answers. "It's a house for a mouse." Devon exclaims. "I think there's a hippo inside," says Stephie. Then they start to impress doors and windows and escape holes. Devon removes a chunk of clay and yells, "Ahhh-tootie!" All of the children join in and create a chorus of sounds. I ask what it means, and Devon says that is what you say when you want to take some clay out. And so they continue their chorus of "Ahhh-tootie!" and exploring the unique properties of clay.

Gradually, the children start to pull off little bits of clay and shape them into various things. They roll out snakes and mice and strange-looking animals or creatures. They make up stories as they work, saying, "This mouse lives inside the clay and wants to get back in." Or "This is a dinosaur and this is his house." Some children will often play and explore the clay block for as long as an hour at a time.

The children start to work with smaller pieces of clay, shaping it into their own separate figures. They have no problem deciding what to make. In Figure 4.12, Jeremy creates a centipede, saying, "It's trying to escape from something. I haven't quite figured it out yet." And he continues to apply strips of clay over the top, making a type of cage.

There are many different kinds of clay to use. Air-dry clay dries by itself and can be painted with watercolors or acrylic paints. Model Magic also air dries but not as hard and can also be painted. Ceramic clay needs to be fired in a kiln. Oil-based clay comes under many different names and

Figure 4.12. Jeremy creates his centipede from clay.

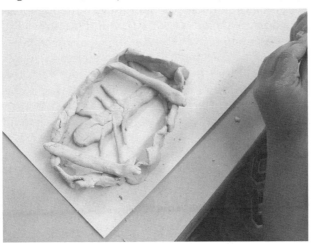

is always moist, but it may be difficult to initially soften it. I usually use it in the winter after I place it on top of a heat source. Sculpey is a clay that can be baked at 275 degrees in a home oven. It's great for making small objects, which young children love to do. There are also many recipes online for making your own clay. Experimenting with different kinds helps children discern the properties unique to each. In my teaching I find that the children love Model Magic because it's so pliable. They also love ceramic clay because of the lasting products it gives them.

Wood

Most children enjoy playing with blocks, and building a wood sculpture is similar to building with blocks, but on a smaller scale. The manipulation of small wooden pieces and other small objects is intriguing for children. I often show pictures of sculptures, but it's more beneficial to view sculptures in person, since children sometimes are unable to imagine what the three-dimensional object is really like. The pictures I do show are usually of large outdoor sculptures shown in their environment, with buildings or trees nearby. That gives the sculptures a scale to which the children can more easily relate. Sometimes I show the children sculptures created by other children, but I normally don't like to do that since I think it channels their thinking into creating something similar.

I have a collection of wood pieces that I bring out occasionally. One day I brought along several small cars, trucks, and little people. We looked at pictures of sculptures in the outdoors and imagined walking through them. I asked the children if they thought they could build a sculpture for the cars and people to drive and walk through (Figure 4.13). In artistic terms, we were discussing *negative space*, or the space between objects or parts of objects. Negative space is an important element in a sculpture or painting. Since the children were too young to understand the concept of how negative space contributes to overall interest in works of art, presenting it in a simple fashion, as a window or door or tunnel through which things or people can pass, is much easier for them to understand, and more developmentally appropriate.

The children created wonderful wood sculptures, using people and cars as props. They told stories about their sculptures and used markers and watercolors to add details.

At a later date, I suggested the children draw a picture of their sculpture. With deep concentration, they carefully observed the different forms as they attempted to draw them. Although their drawings were not completely accurate, I was impressed with their ability to focus and interpret their sculptures in their own way. Some children focused more on the horizontal pieces while others stressed the vertical. They noticed many more shapes and the directions of the forms than I believe they would have if they had drawn someone else's sculpture.

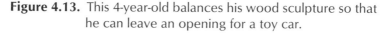

Figure 4.13. This 4-year-old balances his wood sculpture so that he can leave an opening for a toy car.

CONCLUSION

While I have discussed only a few elements of art here, there are several ways to extend them. I have many reproductions of artworks hanging up in my classroom, and the children and I refer to them repeatedly. After a few weeks, I change them and hang up different ones. The children are used to seeing images placed around the room, and often are excited when new ones are there. Practically any artwork can be used to explore color, line, and shape. Even black and white paintings can show differences in values between black and white. Using natural objects along with reproductions gives children a way to compare objects in the real world with objects in a painted world.

Introducing concepts of line, shape, and color also lets children (and teachers) know that not all art activities need to be dependent on areas of the curriculum. There is a body of art knowledge that can be explored on its own.

CHAPTER FIVE

Concepts in the Early Childhood Curriculum

FINDING WORKS OF ART and accompanying lessons to complement and support activities in the preschool curriculum is a simple process. It is easy to search among the numerous art Web sites (listed in Appendix A) to find images to illustrate friends or families, insects, birds, seasons, and others. When works of art are integrated into the curriculum, children become accustomed to seeing a variety of images, increasing their exposure to different styles and artists, and adding to their visual repertoire.

The activities I discuss in this chapter are snapshot views of how one can integrate works of art into the early childhood curriculum. They are certainly not exhaustive. I have selected particular concepts because they are usually the ones that garner the most interest, but there are many more that can be included depending on the direction the children take. The lessons and activities I do with the children usually extend over a period of time with accompanying conversations, activities, and projects.

PEOPLE

One of the first representational drawings that young children create is a person. Children move from scribbling to making lines and circles, to making circles with lines emanating from them, which soon become "tadpole figures," or people (Figure 5.1). Children often draw themselves first, or other family members. Since a large part of a child's world revolves around themselves, their families, and friends, it is a natural progression as a topic for the early childhood classroom. Self-portraits make up a large part of an early lesson, as children explore their individuality and self-esteem. Families and friends are common themes, as well.

Families and Friends

Just as young children are fascinated with other children their age, so they are fascinated with paintings of other children. They immediately identify

Figure 5.1. Laura draws typical "tadpole" figures to represent the members of her family.

with them in one way or another. In one preschool classroom, teachers were discussing families with their children. I brought in two reproductions for us to view, Mary Cassatt's *The Sisters* and William Johnson's *Three Friends*.

I first asked the children, "What do you see?" The replies were varied, depending on the framework of each child. Some of the responses were: "I see two girls, they're sisters!" "I see squares." "I see red and purple." No answer was wrong. As the children responded, they pointed to the various colors, shapes, or objects (Figure 5.2). "What makes you think they're sisters?" I asked about the Cassatt.

> OZZI: They have the same clothes on.
> CAITLIN: Their hair is the same color.
> CM: What about this one. [Points to the William Johnson painting] Do you think they look the same?
> FAYE: No, they have different color skin.
> DARCY: They have different hats on.
> DOMINIC: Their eyes are all the same.

On and on the children talked about the differences and similarities between the two paintings. Then they started talking about their own families—their sisters, brothers, grandparents, and parents. I was learning more about them as they talked. I placed a variety of materials on the table, and they started to draw. As they drew, they talked freely about what

Figure 5.2. Susi points to one of the sisters in Cassatt's painting.

Mary Cassatt, *The Young Girls* © Culture and Sport Glasgow (Museums).

they were creating. Some children worked for 10 minutes, others worked for 40 minutes, depending on their attention span.

Another day I showed reproductions of families. I used a Picasso painting from his blue period and a Henry Moore abstract sculpture of a mother and child. Again the children were immersed in our ensuing conversation. We discussed how Picasso's family portrait was somewhat realistic, but Moore's was abstract. The children remembered these terms and easily distinguished between the abstract and realistic.

The children chose their own materials, such as crayons, markers, oil pastels, cut paper, and so on. Most of my materials are available on open shelves for the children to make choices. I find that young children love to draw with many different materials. They prefer small tools, such as pencils and thin markers and brushes, rather than large tools (Plate 5). The children drew pictures of their families and extended families.

After the children drew, they shared their work with the group, describing their drawings and families (Figure 5.3). Conversations and sharing of artwork is important in that it extends thinking and reflection and shows that we value the children's ideas and perspectives. When I return a class to their regular classroom and the teacher greets the children with "What did you learn in art today?" it lets the children know that their work is important. When a teacher says, "Go put your work in your cubby," without looking at it or responding to it, it sends a message to the children that what they do in art class is not valued.

Figure 5.3. Faye draws people in her family: "We are riding in the car."

Faces and Emotions

One of the preschool teachers was discussing emotions with her children. I decided to support the lesson with several reproductions of portraits that displayed some kind of emotion. The children talked about how they thought the people felt who were depicted in the paintings. Then we discussed several emotions, trying to make our faces change to fit the feelings expressed. We talked about how our faces change depending on how we feel. Carl said that your eyebrows go down if you are mad. Stephie said that your eyebrows go up if you are surprised.

The children were markedly adept at showing various emotions. They were also perceptive about what artists were depicting in their art. They could easily identify several emotions: scared, angry, sad, happy, surprised. In Copley's painting of Paul Revere, they determined that the artist was showing Paul Revere thinking, and they quickly copied the look (Figure 5.4; Plate 6). They had great fun showing the different emotions and were eager to demonstrate them for their classmates (Figure 5.5). In a subsequent activity about animals, some of the children continued the emotion theme by depicting dogs and cats looking happy or mad.

As the children began painting and drawing people showing emotions, they talked about things that made them happy or sad (Plate 7). Carl said that he was going to draw a picture of himself with an angry look, because sometimes his brother made him angry (Figure 5.6). Another child described

Figure 5.4. Aaron demonstrates his thinking pose, inspired
by Copley's Paul Revere.

his drawing as embarrassed, which I thought was a little sophisticated for
a 4-year-old. There was a range of emotions (Figure 5.7), although not all
of them were representational. Some younger children drew simple tadpole figures, and then covered them up with a range of colors. As they
worked they described the feelings they were trying to depict.

Figure 5.5. Laura shows us her scared look. I was surprised at how clearly
the children expressed being scared.

Figure 5.6. Carl draws himself with an angry look.

I think it's important to stress with children that the drawings or paintings they do are all different; some may be realistic, and others may be nonobjective. If one child says another's work is "just a scribble," I say, "Yes, it is! Look how the lines go around and around!" I remind them of all the artwork they have seen, and that not all of it is realistic. Some children may depict a feeling with scribbles of color or movement of a tool on the paper rather than a realistic rendition. Sometimes we just don't

Figure 5.7. Nate draws people who are sad and surprised.

know the intention of the artist, and that's OK as well. I remind the children that they are all different people with different ideas, so their artwork will be different too. I also make sure that we all share our artwork with each other, pointing out the interesting aspects of each.

THE MANUFACTURED WORLD

We live in a world where "things" are all around us, from cars, computers, and video games to our homes, eating tools, dishes, and toys. The manufactured world is a large part of our lives, and children are exposed to it constantly. It is a part of art as well, and artists often use it as a theme in their work. Sometimes architecture is a theme; sometimes artists use patterns they find in shadows, or manhole covers, or brickwork. The list is endless. I only discuss a few themes here, but by now it should be evident that any theme can be supported with a variety of visual reproductions and accompanying activity.

Transportation

I like to do transportation themes with the children because at first it seems like a narrow topic. But as the children discuss how people and things move, the topic is almost limitless. We start by discussing how they go to school, how they go to visit their grandparents or friends, and how they go to the store. They often come up with many different ways of transporting themselves: walking; skating; riding in the car, bus, train, airplane, or subway; riding a horse, skateboard, or bicycle.

   In one classroom the children were learning about transportation, specifically trains. Their teachers were taking them on an actual train ride. To prepare for this experience, the children learned about different kinds of trains, what they looked like, what they sounded like, who traveled on trains, and so on. As the art specialist visiting the classroom, I showed the children two reproductions of paintings depicting trains, a surreal Magritte, *Time Transfixed*, and a slightly more realistic Paul Delvaux, *Trains du Soir* (Figure 5.8). We talked briefly about the paintings:

   CM: Let's look at these paintings. What do you see?
   SHERRI: I see trains. And a little girl here [she points to the lower
      right corner of the painting].
   CM: What do you think the little girl is doing?
   SHERRI: She's going to get on the train. Yes, she's going to visit her
      Grandma.

Figure 5.8. Sheila points to Magritte's painting.

Rene Magritte, *Time Transfixed* © 2009 C. Herscovici, London / Artists
Rights Society (ARS), New York. Paul Delvaux, *Trains du Soir* © 2009
Artists Rights Society (ARS), New York / SABAM, Brussels.

ADAM: [Interjects] The train is coming out of the fireplace! It's
    coming into the house. I think Santa is bringing the train.
AIMEE: It's nighttime. I can see the moon! I don't like to go out at
    nighttime.

The children chattered among themselves and continued to talk en-
thusiastically about the trains. Each child had a different perspective: Sherri
was concerned about what the little girl was doing, Adam thought Santa
was bringing a gift, and Aimee was concerned about the nighttime. Our
conversation turned into storytelling and an imaginative romp through the
children's lives. They were eager to share their experiences with me and
with each other. The children were engaged in storytelling, in exploring
their imaginations, in sharing their experiences with each other.

The children were learning several things through this exposure and
accompanying conversation. They were learning about each other and how
they have different responses to artworks. They were also learning respect
for each other's voices by taking turns in their speaking. They were learning how different artists create in different ways and, in addition, how to
visually read a work of art. One of the first steps to becoming visually lit-
erate is being able to describe what you see in a work of art. The children

Figure 5.9. Nate chooses paper and then uses markers to draw the details on his train.

were well on their way to doing this. I was learning as well, about their lives, their thoughts, and their ideas.

After our discussion, the children collected paper, glue, markers, and other materials. They created their own trains (Figures 5.9 and 5.10), or they created pictures of the dark nighttime. It was their choice. As they worked, the conversation extended to more stories about nighttime, or visiting grandparents, or traveling to different places. Some children made train sounds and banged their markers on the table along with their chanting. They were having a wonderful time!

On another day the children and I brainstormed about different kinds of transportation. Usually they are quick to mention cars, trucks, trains, airplanes, and other common forms. Then we try to get inventive. I will ask them silly questions, such as "Could you ride a chair?" or "Could you ride a block of wood?" or "Could you take a magic carpet ride?" Gradually they catch on and start to think more creatively. Now they are riding tigers, balloons, kites, the wind, and even taking piggyback rides! Then they

Figure 5.10. Khoury uses cut paper, yarn, and markers to show his train.

really push their thinking to transporting objects other than people. How do insects travel? How do seeds travel? They are using their imaginative and critical thinking skills and telling stories all at the same time (Egan, 1999). Who knew that transportation was such a large and varied topic?

The transportation theme can be extended in several ways. In the example above, the children explored trains in depth. From there, they could explore where trains travel to, what they see from the windows of a train, who works on trains, or patterns they see on trains. Any other method of travel could be explored in depth as well and can branch off into other areas. Exploring how seeds travel can lead to birds, wind, and weather and how seeds germinate and grow.

Architecture

Another topic the children and I discuss often is architecture. Since children love to talk about their homes and the buildings in which their parents work, that's where we usually begin. We discuss the different rooms—their bedrooms, their favorite rooms—and what their families do in them. I show them van Gogh's painting of his bedroom in Arles, and the children compare it to theirs. Then we move on to other forms of architecture, the shapes of the windows and doors and the views we see from them. We look at and discuss stores: grocery stores, toy stores, and clothing stores. We look at reproductions of cities, farms, houses, tents, adobe houses, castles, and architecture from many different cultures. Children are amazed to see that there are so many different kinds of homes around the world. They also like to talk about visiting the homes of their friends and relatives, since they are often different from their own.

When we talk about their homes, I help them walk through them for an exercise in visual recall. The children are curious about what my home looks like, and so I describe it to them, trying to use lots of descriptive words. I close my eyes and think out loud, as I describe what I see. I mention driving up to my house, my driveway, the trees and stone walls I pass. I might describe one of the rooms inside, the windows, the furniture, ceiling fan, and so on. Then the children do the same. They are curious and ask many questions.

Sometimes we draw or paint rooms and buildings (Figure 5.11). Other times we build them out of wood, boxes, or other three-dimensional materials. Often the children will use paper to create three-dimensional rooms in their imaginary or realistic houses. They love folding and bending the paper so that it "sticks up" from the surface.

Any of the topics we explore in architecture has the potential to veer off in another direction. For example, when discussing grocery stores one

Figure 5.11. Aaron draws a picture of his bedroom. He points to the dresser and says, "This is where I keep my clothes."

day, the conversation turned to food, and so we discussed our favorite foods and where we might find them. I mentioned my favorite breakfast of blueberries and cereal, and the children shared their favorite foods with me. Stephie liked chocolate-chip cookies, Bobby liked tomato soup, and Sheila liked Skittles. We looked at paintings and sculptures of food, drew pictures of them (Plate 8), and created them out of clay (Figure 5.12).

It's important to be flexible when working with young children because it's difficult to predict what will capture their interest in any one moment. If you are prepared for anything, the children will be enriched because they will have a greater interest in the topic at hand. I believe it is not best practice to have a scripted plan for an activity. There should be lots of options.

Another time during our discussion of architecture, the conversation turned to toy stores, and children began talking about their favorite toys and stuffed animals. So, of course, that's what they wanted to draw! They drew pictures of their favorite teddy bears or their favorite toy cars or trains. Sometimes the children drew them all lined up as in a toy store, other times they drew them separately.

THE NATURAL WORLD

The natural world has endless areas to explore and children talk about what they have found in it constantly: birds, insects, puddles, waves on the beach, or leaves on the trees in their backyards. As a child, I was fascinated by

Figure 5.12. Rachel and Stephie make delicious chocolate-chip cookies out of different kinds of clay.

nature and explored trees and wildflowers every day, trying to identify them. Most children, if given the opportunity, will do the same.

Animals

A common topic for children is animals, and they all seem to have a favorite. After discussing human emotions one year, we looked at several reproductions of animals, one of them Edward Hicks's *The Peaceable Kingdom*. We talked about how the children thought the animals in the painting felt. They were quite perceptive about the expressions on the animals' faces. Some of the children said they looked scared or surprised, others said they looked friendly. They identified many of the animals, and we discussed animal personalities. They knew that lions were brave, and lambs were cuddly and gentle. They discussed the pets they had, and many of them had dogs or cats. I then showed them *Country Dog Gentlemen*, a painting by Roy de Forest, who creates many paintings and sculptures of dogs.

I was surprised to find that the children loved his painting. Although I thought some of the dog expressions were scary, the children did not. I asked the children what they saw in the painting.

> STEVEN: They're wild dogs because they have red eyes.
> SHERRI: I see spots on the dog's tongue because the artist can do whatever he wants.

ELISE: I like the dog that has hair [although several children did not like this dog].

DANIEL: I like the dog with the ears sticking up.

ELISE: I don't like the dog that has spots.

JILL: The one I like is the one that has paws on his eyes and spots on his tongue. That other one is a seal. Oh, no, it's a dog, I see his ear.

The children talked on and on about dogs they had or other people's dogs. They knew several breeds. Jeremy suddenly said, "Remember Blue Dog?" About a month prior, I had read *Why Is Blue Dog Blue?* (Rodrigue & Goldstone, 2002), which is about the blue dog paintings by George Rodrigue. We had also looked at several of his paintings. The children all remembered looking at the pictures, and I brought out new ones to show them since I had recently visited an exhibit of the paintings in New Orleans.

When I asked the children why the artist would paint dogs that way, Sherri replied, "The artist can do whatever they want. If they want to paint that way, they can." And so the children painted and drew their dogs and animals any way they wanted too!

After Nate drew his picture of dogs (Figure 5.13), he began intently drawing lots of colored circles below them. He talked as he drew, saying, "These are lots of dogs with colored stones in front. They are rainbow rocks." When another child asked him what rainbow rocks were, he replied, "They are rocks with lots of colors in them." What an apt descrip-

Figure 5.13. Nate draws lots of dogs with his "rainbow rocks" in front of them.

tion of them, I thought to myself, and it could be another avenue to explore in an additional activity.

Stephie's dog (Figure 5.14) is much different from Noah's. She worked on this drawing for quite a while, pausing to reflect on the marks she made. After each pause, she would add something else. Finally, she added lots of bows to the legs, tail, and body and announced, "I'm done!"

Birds

We have many birdfeeders at my school so the children watch and learn about them every day. I am also interested in birds, and have many pictures and videos I have taken of hummingbirds, finches, orioles, and others, which I share with the children.

In Chapter 3, I discussed looking at reproductions of birds and the ensuing conversations. There are several others that children enjoy looking at, such as Morris Graves's *Wounded Gull*, Aboriginal prints of birds, and African sculptures. I try to include lots of different cultural portrayals of animals, and we discuss how some animals serve different purposes in other places around the world. I have a collection of stuffed birds that play recordings of the actual birdcall when pressed, and I also bring in bird nests for the children to look at and see what's inside.

One day I brought in a nest from an Eastern Phoebe. The bird had already had two broods so the nest was vacant. Eastern Phoebes often build their nest in the same place as in the previous year, which is usually over

Figure 5.14. Stephie's dog is dressed in fancy bows.

my front door. They have one brood, and when that brood fledges, they proceed to build another nest on top of the first one, kind of like a double-decker! During the first incubation, I found an egg on the ground and did not know where it had come from, so I carefully placed it in the phoebe's nest next to three others that were there, hoping it would hatch. I initially did not find out whether the egg hatched along with the others. However, when I finally took the vacant nest down and peeled away the top layer, I saw that the egg was still inside, never having hatched. The children loved this story and gingerly touched the egg. Needless to say, they created many nests and birds with different drawing materials and clay (Figure 5.15).

Plants

Plants, flowers, shells, and leaves are abundant and easy to collect for exploration. Seasons are a large part of the early childhood curriculum, and teachers help children learn about the changes that take place as one season progresses to another. Reproductions that show the different seasons in landscapes, seascapes, and cityscapes abound.

In one lesson with plants I brought in iris leaves, which the children placed on top of a van Gogh reproduction. We compared the differences between the real leaves and the painted ones. The children looked at the different colors, brushstrokes, and textures (Figure 5.16).

Figure 5.15. Heidi's collage shows a birdhouse with a flag on top. She includes a little white perch using a pipe cleaner on the house, birds flying around it, and, of course, a happy sun.

Figure 5.16. Preschoolers point to shapes and colors in one of van Gogh's paintings.

Texture is a difficult concept for young children to understand. Bringing in actual leaves and having the children feel them and compare them to those in the painting helped them understand the idea of real texture as opposed to implied texture, as in the van Gogh.

I also brought in pieces of bark from various trees, and the children explored the texture by feeling it, doing crayon rubbings of it, and then drawing it. We looked carefully at the lines and colors on the different pieces, naming all the colors and lines that we saw. The children were surprised to see oranges, yellows, and even different shades of purple in the bark. They carefully tried to duplicate what they saw. Then we did the same with leaves. The children did a few leaf rubbings, but also drew the lines and colors. Then we gathered all the different textures together and formed them into one large tree that was displayed in the classroom.

THE IMAGINARY WORLD

I show several reproductions every day, and I am usually prepared with some kind of plan, but I let the children's interests guide me. I often alter my plan because the children may suddenly become enthusiastic about a new idea or topic. One day I showed reproductions of paintings that told a story, such as David's *Oath of the Horatii*. The children loved hearing the story of the three triplets going to battle another set of triplets. It is really an impressive, classical painting, and they had a grand time trying to figure out what the story was all about.

At the same time, I showed them some of Keith Haring's works. Haring started out with chalk drawings on subway walls in New York. Many of his figures are bright, graphic renditions of people in different settings. When people asked what Haring was drawing, he would say that he was only the artist, they had to come up with the story! The children loved this concept and told elaborate, nonsensical stories of what they thought his paintings were about. When I showed the same pictures to older children, they were not nearly as imaginative or inventive.

In Figure 5.17 Carl describes his collage to Marc: "Once upon a time there were three men trying to find a treasure. They went this way." He proceeded to point out the path they took and where the treasures were. Then he changed his mind and said, "Oh, no, there are four men trying to find a treasure, but it's really nothing. It's invisible gold!" He had great fun sharing his story with the class, and all the children listened intently and laughed along with him.

I had worked with Michael for several months before I discovered that he was a master storyteller. After looking at pictures that tell stories, Michael worked on a drawing for 2 weeks. Here is his description: "There's this dog named Dogzilla, and he's hilarious. I learned the names from the Dav Pilkey [1993] books. There are two explorers who drive in their car on animal patrol. Their friends are news reporter dogs, and the police are after them. They don't like why they are cutting down trees. They

Figure 5.17. Carl explains his story to Marc.

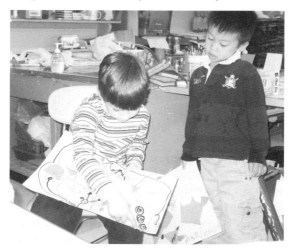

are all dogs." Michael was delighted with this story, and all of the children gathered around him and were transfixed by his humorous descriptions. Here was a perfect example of how to foster imaginative and critical thinking skills (Egan, 1999; Greene, 2001).

When the children were drawing dogs and other animals one day, Susi was intent on her work. She drew one enormous dog with six legs. Then she drew all sorts of shapes and lines around it. Here is her description: "My big dog is in a house. It is a princess doggie. This is the door to the house. But, guess what? It changes into a TV, and then it changes into a refrigerator!" Ah, I thought to myself, this is why this is my favorite part of the day. These children were so inventive, creating story after story. They had no qualms about changing their minds and altering the story to find a better fit.

LETTERS AND NUMBERS

One common part of an early childhood curriculum is to introduce letters and numbers to the children. There are many exemplary artists who use letters and numbers in their paintings or sculptures so it is the perfect opportunity to show different styles in art. In one lesson, I showed the children artwork of Jasper Johns and Charles Demuth. Johns has some wonderful paintings using letters and numbers, and Demuth has a beautiful abstract painting titled *The Figure Five in Gold*, based on a poem by William Carlos Williams.

The children had fun looking for different numbers and letters in the artworks, and we briefly discussed the artists and why they would paint that way. The Johns painting was particularly intriguing to them because many of the numbers appear to be hidden within other numbers. The children would shout, "I see a 2! I see a 5!" They traced the numbers with their fingers.

I provided several short strips of colored paper and the children were free to cut up their own shapes. The children loved manipulating the paper strips and could easily make letters and numbers. They played with them for quite a while. They then glued the strips on another larger piece of paper. Some of the children glued down the strips all over the paper, with no regard for figures. Others shaped their strips into letters or numbers and glued them down in an orderly manner. Paints and crayons were available for them to add to the compositions. I suggested that they paint around their paper strips, but the children had their own ideas (Plate 9).

There were many different responses. Some children created legible numbers in their compositions, whereas other children delighted in the

Figure 5.18. Katie is using the end of her brush to make marks.

tactile qualities of the paint, making marks and mixing colors, depending on their developmental readiness. Children also drew with the ends of their brushes to make additional marks on their papers (Figure 5.18). Some children noticed how the marks changed colors depending on the color paper they used. Other children scribbled on their paintings and noticed how the marks changed. One 3-year-old was intrigued with the color blue and painted her hands instead (Figure 5.19; Plate 10). Embedded in this activ-

Figure 5.19. Nell decides to paint her hands before she paints her paper!

ity was a new way of looking at art, one that sees painting not as representational, but as an object worthy of existing by itself, an important twentieth-century contribution to the visual arts. Also embedded in the activity were how artists use media, how colors change, and how different tools can make different marks.

CONCLUSION

Although some of these scenarios are brief, they set the stage for a more in-depth examination of curricular ideas. Any idea can veer off in a different direction. The important thing is to be flexible, listen to the children, and be willing to accept all interpretations. When I was a beginning teacher, I was more focused on how the final project looked. Now I know that that is not the important issue. What the children learn by discussing works of art and sharing stories with their classmates is more important. Their interpretation of a work is valid, and their choices for how to interpret a follow-up activity are also valid.

CHAPTER SIX

The Next Steps

I HAVE PRESENTED many ways to connect looking at and learning about art with basic art concepts and activities in the early childhood classroom. However, education doesn't stop there. We, as teachers, need to educate parents, caregivers, and families about methods to extend this learning at home.

Early childhood teachers are quite adept at communicating with parents about their child's activities. For many parents of young children, this is the first time their child is away from home. They want to know what they have missed, and they want to hear the particulars of the day. It is the perfect opportunity to communicate with them. Not only do we need to communicate about what their children have done each day, but also about best practice. It is in the children's best interest to do that, and doing so educates parents and guardians as well.

Traditionally, it is the child who has benefited from home and school connections. The fact that parents and guardians might benefit has been seen as secondary (Seefeldt, 1985). But making a home and school connection is of the utmost importance since children's home environments have such a large impact on their lives.

EXTENDING LEARNING FROM SCHOOL TO HOME

There are several ways to communicate with families about children's art experiences. A good way to begin is to send home a letter early in the year, describing your approach to art with young children. I normally do this the second week of school. I share basic facts of creating with young children, and I offer suggestions for ways families can help support their children's learning. See Appendix B for a sample letter that is easily adaptable for any teaching situation.

Children may not always produce a product in the classroom. They may sometimes just have a conversation about reproductions or about art in general as they explore different materials. Document these activities by photographing the children interacting and experimenting. Parents and children both love to look at photographs. Jot down snippets of conversations to include with the photos, and post them in a well-trafficked area.

When children do produce a product, write a brief description of it and include the names of any artists you might have used to accompany the activity. You might provide ideas for follow-up activities or new vocabulary you used with the children. Photocopy your description and tape it onto the back or bottom of the work before sending it home. This way, you will be educating the families as well, and they can continue the conversation in the home.

Display the children's artwork in the classroom and in other areas of the school, if possible. Also hang up accompanying reproductions with it to educate parents and other faculty about what your children are learning.

Invite families into the classroom to assist in a project or activity. This gives you the opportunity to model developmentally appropriate behavior and conversations, as well as to share art knowledge parents and guardians may not have. In addition, family members or relatives may have a particular hobby or work-related art interest they would be willing to share with children. Careers in art take many forms, from graphic arts to product or package design, to textiles, illustration, or Web design. Letting children know, even at a young age, that there are several ways in which the visual arts contribute to our culture as well as to other cultures sets the stage for developing a supportive attitude toward art in the future.

EXTENDING LEARNING THROUGH TAKE-HOME ACTIVITIES

Several years ago a colleague and I designed a take-home portfolio project for young children (Mulcahey, 2002). My colleague wanted to learn more about art, and I wanted to learn more about young children, so our collaboration was beneficial for both of us.

One of my goals in designing the portfolios was to show parents another way of thinking about art so they could begin to do that with their children. Providing questions about artwork and the work the children were creating would model appropriate types of questioning techniques for parents.

The portfolio contained several small reproductions of artworks, sample questions to generate thinking about and reflection on the works of art, and a collection of art materials for children and their families to explore. We also included a notebook for comments on or questions about the project.

The response to the project was overwhelmingly supportive. Children loved taking home the portfolio for a week, and families responded positively in the notebook. While this project was initially time-consuming to set up, the benefits outweighed the hours of initial design. It was an ideal way to forge a strong home-school connection. And a cooperative collaboration between home and school has shown to dramatically raise educational productivity (Tizard, Schofield & Hewison, 1982).

While you may not initially have enough time to design your own take-home portfolio, it can be done on a smaller scale. When you send home children's artwork, you can include sample questions on the back for families to ask their children. You might suggest asking the child to tell them a story about the drawing or painting, or perhaps have the child demonstrate how the work was created. Any comments that provide further interaction between parents or guardians and children will support the young child's interest in art.

You could also photocopy a small reproduction and send that home with a few questions to generate conversation and interest. In Jean Dallaire's *Birdy* (refer to Figure 3.1), for example, you might suggest asking families to engage in a conversation about the various objects in the work. They might ask, "Why do you think the artist painted the bird that way?" or "Why do you think the artist painted a small plane at the top?" Any divergent question can generate thinking and storytelling.

Another way to help provide activities for at-home learning is to suggest fun scavenger hunts. Children, with the help of a more capable peer or adult, can look for interesting textures or colors in natural or manufactured objects, do backyard bird counts and drawings, look at and draw different lines or shapes around the home, or bring in objects of a certain color. Send home a piece of paper with a hole in it so children and families can look through it for a different perspective. These results can then be explored in the classroom. How many different shades of red did all the children find? A painting activity of the different reds could follow. How many different kinds of lines exist in the home? Can the children make up other kinds of lines? What did the children see when they looked through the hole in the paper? All of these simple activities generate thinking and make the families more aware of their environment and its relation to the basic building blocks of art.

Invite parents and guardians to send in interesting materials, such as plants, shells, stones, and other natural objects, or manufactured articles with interesting patterns and textures. Because the children have ownership of the objects they bring in, they will be more excited about learning about and sharing their small treasures with their classmates.

CONCLUSION

The ideas I have presented in this book are only some of many that I use with young children. My favorite part of my teaching is listening to them discuss the artworks we view, their interpretations of them, and the stories they tell. It provides a window into their lives, one that teachers are not always privileged to look through. Of course I'm interested in the artwork they create, but it's a result of our rich conversations.

It is my hope that you will begin or continue to use works of art in your classroom and home. I love using art with children and cannot think of a more enjoyable way to interact. It's enjoyable because I learn so much from the children. When I was studying for my PhD, I did a pilot study with 6th graders. I met with a group of them for several weeks, and we engaged in a series of conversations about a collection of their artwork. I mainly wanted to listen to them interact and tell stories about drawings they had done over a period of 6 years. I asked them lots of questions and listened intently as they laughed, told stories, and interacted with each other. After a few weeks, one of them said to me, "You're acting like we are the experts; we are the experts on our lives." I don't remember what I said at that point. But I have always remembered that remark.

As you explore the world of art with your children, listen to their stories and take your cues from them. Their infectious enthusiasm and creativity will be your guide in designing rich follow-up activities. Listen to the children for they are the experts on their lives.

Art Resources

THE APPROACH I PRESENT in this book requires a collection of art re-productions. High-quality reproductions can be purchased from many sources, but there are other ways to collect them. Many Web sites allow you to print out reproductions, or bring up images to view. Out-of-date calendars are a good and inexpensive source of artwork. Oversize art books from libraries provide even more variety. For a well-balanced cur-riculum, you will need a rich and varied collection of art reproductions from different time periods, different cultures, different styles, and dif-ferent artists, including women and minorities. Include reproductions of paintings, collages, photographs, prints, sculptures, ceramics, textiles, and advertisements.

Do not limit your selections to the artists or kinds of artwork that you like. This is putting your biases on others, and children should be able to make their own decisions about their likes and dislikes. Arcim-baldo is not one of my favorite artists, but when I showed a group of kindergarten children some of his works, they loved them. The conver-sations we had and the stories the children told were creative and thought provoking.

Try to introduce many different styles of artworks to your children. Children love contemporary art, which often incorporates many varied materials, not just paint, paper, or other traditional two- and three-dimensional media. Use work that you don't understand, and you can discover along with your children. Children are surprisingly perceptive and open to different ways of looking at the world.

To get you started on your journey, here is a list of artists and works, organized by theme. The list is not exhaustive; that would entail another book! I also list several good Web sites for viewing images.

THEMES AND ARTISTS

People

SELF-PORTRAITS AND PORTRAITS

Frida Kahlo
Alice Neel
Rembrandt
Kitagawa Utamaro

Most artists have created self-portraits at one time or another. Any of the Web sites listed at the end of this appendix, or a Google search, will find several more self-portraits.

FRIENDS AND FAMILIES

Mary Cassatt
William Johnson
Pablo Picasso, several different realistic and abstract portraits
Carmen Lomas Garza, Mexican home life and celebrations

FACES AND EMOTIONS

Max Beckman, expressive self-portraits
Frida Kahlo
Edvard Munch
Picasso
Gargoyle sculptures

The Manufactured World

TRANSPORTATION

Arthur G. Dove, *The Train*, 1934
Rene Magritte, *Time Transfixed*
Paul Delvaux, *Trains du Soir*
Egon Schiele, paintings of boats
Franz Marc, abstract paintings of horses
Edgar Degas, paintings of racehorses
Winslow Homer, paintings of ships at sea

Frederic Remington, paintings of horses and cowboys of the American West

ARCHITECTURE

Frank Lloyd Wright
Antoni Gaudi
Louis Sullivan
Eero Saarinen
Le Corbusier
Zaha Kadid (first woman to win the Pritzker Prize, architecture's highest award)
Photographs of architecture from different cultures
Paintings and collages of buildings, cities, and other types of dwellings

Also see architecture Web site below.

The Natural World

ANIMALS

Deborah Butterfield, sculptures of horses
Cave paintings
Currier and Ives
Roy de Forest, paintings of dogs
Edward Hicks
Pable Picasso, bull prints
Edgar Degas, paintings of horses
Arthur G. Dove, *Cow and Fence* (*Bull*), undated
Gwen Knight, *Running Horse*, 1999
Serge Lemonde, humorous close-ups of animals
Andy Warhol, prints of endangered animals

BIRDS

Jean Dallaire, *Birdy*
Currier and Ives, *The Happy Family*
Alexander Calder, *Only Only Bird*, 1951
Morris Graves, *Wounded Gull*, 1943
Karl Knaths, *Duck Decoy*, 1931

Vincent van Gogh, *Wheat Field with Crows*
Frida Kahlo, *The Frame*
Keiichi Nishimura, *Cranes over Moon* (and other paintings of cranes)
Marsden Hartley, *Chanties to the North*
Ancient Egyptian and African sculptures of birds
Pudlo Pudlat (Inuit artist)

PLANTS

Henri Rousseau, paintings
Kai Chan, sculptures and installations constructed from natural materials
Andy Goldsworthy, site-specific sculptures using natural, on-site materials
Georgia O'Keefe
Piet Mondrian

OCEAN LIFE

Winslow Homer
Paul Klee, *Fish Magic, The Golden Fish*
Cristoforo de Predis, *The End of the World and the Last Judgement: "The fish will be above the sea."*
Seitei Watanabe, *Crayfish*
Malcah Zeldis, *Fish*

SEASONS AND WEATHER

Jennifer Bartlett
David Hockney
Winslow Homer
Impressionist paintings of seasons and weather

The Imaginary World

Marc Chagall
Keith Haring
Red Grooms
Sandy Skoglund, installations
Magritte
Salvador Dali

Food

Wayne Thiebaud
Claes Oldenburg, sculptures of food
Isabel Bishop, *Lunch Counter*, ca. 1940
Mary Ann Currier
Paul Cezanne, still paintings of fruit
Giuseppe Arcimboldo, imaginative paintings of portraits using fruits,
    vegetables, and other objects

Letters and Numbers

Stuart Davis
Charles Demuth
Jasper Johns
Ed Ruscha

Patterns

Betty LaDuke
Aboriginal art
Piet Mondrian
Paul Klee
M. C. Escher
Kenojuak (Ashevak), *Sun Owl and Foliage*
Islamic art, geometric patterns
Gee's Bend quilts

ART WEB SITES

http://architecture.about.com/od/architectsaz/Great_Architects_AZ.htm
    Alphabetical listing of famous architects

http://www.artnet.com
    Search by artist.

http://webmuseum.meulie.net/wm/paint/auth/
    Search by artist.

http://scholarsresource.com/
    Search by artist, museum, type of art, period, or country.

http://www.wga.hu/index.html
   Search European artists by name, title of artwork, or period.

http://www.barewalls.com/index_artist.html
   Search by artist, style, or subject.

http://www.artres.com/c/htm/Home.aspx
   Search by subject, artist, or keyword.

http://www.phillipscollection.org/research/american_art/index.htm
   Search by artist, medium, or date.

http://www.ccca.ca/artists/artist_info.html?link_id=183
   Features the work of Kai Chan, who uses natural objects to build sculptures.

http://www.artcyclopedia.com
   Search by artist, title of work, movement, or art museum.

http://www.metmuseum.org/
   Holdings of the Metropolitan Museum of Art in New York City.

http://hirshhorn.si.edu/
   Modern and contemporary art in the Hirshhorn collection in Washington, DC.

http://www.nmai.si.edu/
   A collection of Native American art and artifacts.

http://www.nmafa.si.edu/voice.html
   Holdings of the National Museum of African Art.

http://www.asia.si.edu/
   Asian art and a specialized collection of American art.

http://www.uwrf.edu/history/women.html
   Lists 700 important women artists from the ninth to the twentieth century.

http://www.museumsyndicate.com/index.php
   Search by artist, country, museum, or date.

Sample Letter to Families

Dear Parents and Guardians,

I would like to welcome you to a new school year. I am your child's art teacher, and I will visit with your child once a week in his or her classroom. Together we will learn about many different artists; we will use a variety of materials; and we will create wonderful things with our ideas and imaginations.

An important part of the art education your child receives is based on exploration, experimentation, and discovery as children manipulate materials and ideas. Young children are "manipulating" tools, and they are often not trying to make something realistic or representational, nor do they have the skills for that. They like to "make marks" and see what their physical actions have created. They might make marks based on how things make them feel or how things smell. They may just enjoy the kinesthetic motion of drawing or scribbling. Scribbling is appropriate for children and will eventually lead to decoding letters and numbers. Children's visual perceptions of the world are different from that of an adult and they are not ready to draw the same way an adult would. They enjoy the process of creation and do not worry about the end product. Your support of these concepts will help provide self-confidence in your child's emerging artistic abilities.

An equally important part of your child's art experience is the response received from families and teachers about your child's work. To make your child's art experience complete, I am asking for your help in the following ways:

- When your child brings home a piece of artwork—be it a scribble, abstract shapes, or a carefully planned composition—try to comment on the elements used in the work. Some things you might mention are the colors used (light, dark, bright; red, orange, and so on), the kinds or numbers of lines and shapes you can see (squiggly lines, short and long lines), the way a tool is used (a lot of pressure or a little), textures (rough, smooth, bumpy), the direction of a line (up, down), or the different brushstrokes used. Avoid asking "What is it?" because this implies that you don't know and that the child has failed to accurately represent something. The children are proud of the marks they make, and they are even prouder when families support their efforts.

- Display your child's artwork in a visible area. Seeing a painting or drawing set apart from other things gives the child a feeling of pride and a sense of satisfaction. Try not to compare it to other children's work. Each child is unique and we all see the world differently.
- Save a variety of your child's work in a portfolio. Artwork is probably the only lasting artifact of the early childhood years, and it provides a unique record of your child's development and personality. Your child and you will enjoy looking through the collection in later years.
- Provide your child with a variety of materials to explore at home. Blank paper, crayons, markers, pastels, scissors, and pencils are a few basic supplies to have available. An unstructured environment is best since the child can experiment and explore independently. You can add other materials from time to time such as clay, string, watercolors, pipe cleaners, and fabric so that your child has many choices. Refrain from providing coloring books or precut shapes, which tells children that they need to rely on adult-created images. They will learn more about themselves and about art if they create their own lines, shapes, and images.
- Engage your child in conversation about his or her artwork if your child is receptive. Talking about the work models adult language and builds self-esteem. Again, talk about the elements your child has used, how the work makes you feel, or use the artwork as a departure point for an imaginary adventure or story.
- Borrow art books from the library or find calendars or postcards with a variety of art reproductions on them. This will support what I do with them in the classroom and will broaden their exposure to different kinds of art.
- Join your child in a quiet exploration of materials and ideas. This will model artistic behavior and will build an artistic relationship. When a child sees his or her parent (guardian) involved in artistic discovery, it strengthens the value of working visually rather than verbally.

I hope these ideas are helpful for you. Please feel free to stop in the art room for a visit or to view the exciting projects all of the children are doing. Together we can provide a meaningful art experience for your child.

Sincerely,

References

Barrett, T. (1997). *Talking about student art*. Worcester, MA: Davis Publications.

Bredekamp, S., & Copple, C. (Eds.). (1997). *Developmentally appropriate practice in early childhood programs* (Rev. ed.). Washington, DC: National Association for the Education of Young Children.

Bruner, J (1962). *On knowing. Essays for the left hand*. Cambridge, MA: Harvard University Press.

Burnham, R. (1994). If you don't stop, you don't see anything. *Teachers College Record, 95*(4), 520–525.

Caine, G., & Caine, R. (1994). *Making connections: teaching and the human brain*. New York: Addison Wesley.

Cannon, J. (1993). *Stellaluna*. Orlando, FL: Harcourt Brace.

Colbert, C., & Taunton, M. (1990). *Discover art: Kindergarten*. Worcester, MA: Davis.

Davis, J. (1993). Museum games. *Teaching, Thinking and Problem Solving, 15*(2), 1–6.

Davis, J. (2005). *Framing education as art: The octopus has a good day*. New York: Teachers College Press.

Dewey, J. (1980). *Art as experience*. New York: Perigee Books. (Original work published 1934)

Donaldson, M. (1978). *Children's Minds*. New York: W. W. Norton.

Douglas, N., Schwartz, J., & Taylor, J. B. (1981). The relationship of cognitive style of young children and their modes of responding to paintings. *Studies in Art Education, 22*(3), 24–31.

Duncum, P. (2002). Children never were what they were: Perspectives on childhood. In Y. Gaudelius & P. Speirs (Eds.), *Contemporary issues in art education* (pp. 97–107). Upper Saddle River, NJ: Prentice Hall.

Durant, S. R. (1996). Reflections on museum education at Dulwich picture gallery. *Art Education, 49*(5), 15–24.

Edwards, B. (1999) *Drawing on the right side of the brain* (3rd ed.). Boston: J. P. Tarcher.

Edwards, C., Gandini, L., & Forman, G. (Eds.). (1993). *The hundred languages of children: the Reggio Emilia approach to early childhood education*. Norwood, NJ: Ablex.

Egan, K. (1999). *Children's minds, talking rabbits, and clockwork oranges: Essays on education*. New York, NY: Teachers College Press.

Egan, K. (2001). *The cognitive tools of children's imagination.* Alkmaar, Netherlands: Annual European Conference on Quality in Early Childhood Education. (ERIC Document Reproductions Service No. ED469669)

Eisner, E. (1985). Why art in education and why art education. In Getty Center for Education in the Arts (Ed.), *Beyond creating: The place for art in America's schools* (pp. 64–69). Los Angeles: J. Paul Getty Trust.

Eisner, E. (1988). *The role of discipline-based art education in America's schools.* Los Angeles: Getty Center for Education in the Arts.

Eisner, E. (1994). *Cognition and curriculum reconsidered* (2nd ed.). New York: Teachers College Press.

Eisner, E. (2002). *The arts and the creation of mind.* New Haven, CT: Yale University Press.

Epstein, A. S., & Trimis, E. (2002). *Supporting young artists: The development of the visual arts in young children.* High/Scope Press.

Freire, P. (1970). *Pedagogy of the oppressed.* New York: Seabury Press.

Gardner, H. (1990). *Art education and human development.* Los Angeles: Getty Center for Education in the Arts.

Gardner, H., & Winner, E. (1979). The development of metaphoric competence: Implications for humanistic disciplines. In S. Sacks (Ed.), *On metaphor.* Chicago: University of Chicago Press.

Goodman, K. S., Smith, E. B., Meredith, R., & Goodman, Y. M. (1987). *Language and thinking in school: A whole-language curriculum* (3rd ed.). New York: R. C. Owen.

Goodman, N. (1978). *Ways of worldmaking.* Hassocks, UK: Harvester Press.

Greene, M. (1995). *Releasing the imagination.* San Francisco: Jossey-Bass.

Greene, M. (2001). *Variations on a blue guitar.* New York: Teachers College Press.

Greeno, J. G. (1989). A perspective on thinking. *American Psychologist, 44*(2), 134–141.

Hamblen, K. (1984). "Don't you think some brighter colors would improve your painting?" or, constructing questions for art dialogues. *Art Education, 37*(1), 12–14.

Hohmann, M., & Weikart, D. P. (1995). *Educating young children.* Ypsilanti, MI: High/Scope Press.

Housen, A. (1983). *The eye of the beholder: Measuring aesthetic development.* Unpublished doctoral dissertation, Harvard University, Cambridge, MA.

Jeffers, C. (1993). A survey of instructors of art methods classes for preservice elementary teachers. *Studies in Art Education, 34*(4), 233–243.

Johnson, L. (2002). Art-centered approach to diversity education in teaching and learning. *Multicultural Education, 9*(4), 18–21.

Kindler, A. (1996). Myths, habits, research, and policy: The four pillars of early childhood art education. *Arts Education Policy Review, 97*(4), 24–31.

Langer, S. (1942). *Philosophy in a new key.* Cambridge, MA: Harvard University Press.

Lankford, E. L. (1992). *Aesthetics: Issues and inquiry.* Reston, VA: National Art Education Association.

Lim, B. (2004). Aesthetic discourses in early childhood settings: Dewey, Steiner, and Vygotsky. *Early Child Development and Care, 174*(5), 473–486.

Moore, M. (1995). Toward a new liberal learning. *Art Education, 48*(6), 6–13.

Mulcahey, C. (2002). Art appreciation kits for kindergartners and their families. *Young Children, 57*(1), 80–88.

National Academy of Early Childhood Programs. (2005). *Accreditation criteria and procedures: position statement of the National Academy of Early Childhood Programs.* Washington, DC: National Association for the Education of Young Children.

Parsons, M. (1987). *How we understand art: A cognitive developmental account of aesthetic experience.* Cambridge, UK: Cambridge University Press.

Peck, J. (1989). Using storytelling to promote language and literacy development. *The Reading Teacher, 43*(2), 138–141.

Pilkey, D. (1993). *Dogzilla.* San Diego, CA: Harcourt Brace Jovanovich.

Rodrigue, G., & Goldstone, R. (2002). *Why is blue dog blue?* New York, NY: Stewart, Tabori, & Chang.

Savva, A. (2003). Young pupils' responses to adult works of art. *Contemporary Issues in Early Childhood, 4*(3), 300–313.

Schirrmacher, R. (1986). Talking with young children about their art. *Young Children, 41*(5), 3–7.

Seefeldt, C. (1985). Parent involvement: Support or stress? *Childhood Education, 62*(2), 98–102.

Siegler, R. S. (1991). *Children's thinking.* Englewood Cliffs, NJ: Prentice-Hall.

Simpson, J. (1996). Constructivism and connection making in art education. *Art Education, 49*(1), 53–59.

Sylwester, R. (1994). How emotions affect learning. *Educational Leadership, 52*(2), 60–65.

Thompson, C. M. (1990). "I make a mark": The significance of talk in young children's artistic development. *Early Childhood Research Quarterly, 5*(2), 215–232.

Thompson, C., & Bales, S. (1991). "Michael doesn't like my dinosaurs": Conversations in a preschool art class. *Studies in Art Education, 33*(1), 43–55.

Tizard J., Schofield, W. N., & Hewison, J. (1982). Collaboration between teachers and parents in assisting children's reading. *British Journal of Educational Psychology, 52*(1), 1–15.

Vygotsky, L. S. (1978). *Mind in society.* Cambridge, MA: Harvard University Press.

Wellhousen, K. (1993). Eliciting and examining young children's storytelling. *Journal of Research in Childhood Education, 7*(2), 62–66.

Winner, E. (1988). *The point of words: Children's understanding of metaphor and irony.* Cambridge, MA: Harvard University Press.

Index

Barrett, T., 27
Bartlett, Jennifer, 86
Bat project, 20
Beasts of the Sea (Matisse), 32
Beckman, Max, 84
Birds
  and concepts in early childhood
    curriculum, 71–72
  resources about, 85–86
  and talking with children about art, 28–
    30
Birdy (Dallaire), 22, 30, 80, 85
Bishop, Isabel, 87
Blank paper, as intimidating, 16
Blue dog paintings, 70
Blue Horses (Marc), 22
Brancusi, Constantin, 53
Bredekamp, S., 20, 47, 49
Bruner, J., 5
Burnham, R., 5
Butterfield, Deborah, 85

Caine, G., 9
Caine, R., 9
Calder, Alexander, 22, 85
Cannon, J., 20
Cassatt, Mary, 59, 60, 84
Cave paintings, 85
Cezanne, Paul, 87
Chagall, Marc, 86
Chanties to the North (Hartley), 86
Children
  as accepting, 29
  art activities for, 15–26
  examples of art of, 38–42
  as experts on their lives, 81
  introducing works of art to, 2–9
  respect for, 26, 65
  trust of, 20
  See also specific topic
Choicesmaking, 21, 22, 23–24, 26, 33, 48,
    60, 66
Clay
  working in, 8, 43, 45, 49, 53–55
  See also Model Magic
Colbert, C., 26
Coloring books, 18–19
Colors
  children's pictures of, 42
  and concepts in art, 43, 46–47, 49–53,
    57

and concepts in early childhood
    curriculum, 73, 76, 77
  and talking with children about art, 35
  and understanding aesthetics, 11
Compliments, 35
Composition (Arp), 32
Concepts
  in art, 43–57
  in early childhood curriculum, 58–77
  See also specific concept
Configuration (Arp), 7, 48
Constructivism, 4
Control
  and art activities for young children, 15,
    16–17
  and concepts in art, 49
  and talking with children about art, 34
Conversations
  about aesthetics, 11
  and attending to work, 35, 36
  importance of having, 14
  to provide feedback, 33–35
  and responses to creative process, 17
  and teachers' responses when talking
    about art, 16, 17, 27–42
  while children are working, 31–33
Copley, John Singleton, 60, 62
Copple, C., 20, 47, 49
Country Dog Gentlemen (de Forest), 69–70
Cow and Fence (Bull) (Dove), 85
Cow (Calder), 22
Crane over Moon (Nishimura), 86
Crayfish (Watanabe), 86
Creativity
  and art activities for young children, 16, 23
  and concepts in art, 47
  and concepts in early childhood
    curriculum, 66–67
  response to, 17
  and talent, 18
Critical thinking
  and concepts in early childhood
    curriculum, 67, 75
  fostering, 7–8
  and introducing works of art to young
    children, 3
Culture
  and art activities for young children, 26
  and concepts in early childhood
    curriculum, 71
  contribution of arts to, 79

About the Author

Christine Mulcahey is a professor at Rhode Island College, where she is an art specialist at the Henry Barnard Laboratory School, teaching art to children from preschool to fifth grade. She also teaches art education courses at the college and mentors preservice art teachers. She holds a doctorate from the University of Rhode Island/Rhode Island College, and has more than 27 years of teaching experience with children and adults. Her research, which has been presented nationally at NAEA and AERA conferences, focuses on children's perspectives on their artistic learning and viewing the world through multiple perspectives. This book is based on her work with preschoolers and kindergarten children.